EARLY NETHERLANDISH ENGRAVING

c. 1440–1540

Ursula Mayr-Harting

Ashmolean Museum, Oxford
1997

ACKNOWLEDGEMENTS

The Ashmolean Museum would like to thank Mr Nicholas Stogdon for his support over a number of years in the conservation and mounting of the early German and Netherlandish print collections.

I am also personally very grateful to Nicholas Stogdon for his invaluable corrections, advice and encouragement. The errors and misconceptions which remain are entirely my own. I would also like to thank for their help in a number of ways: Martin Kauffmann, Heather MacLennan, Nicholas Mayhew, Anne Steinberg, Jeremy Warren, Robin Weekes, Timothy Wilson, the Photographic Studio at the Ashmolean and my colleagues in the Department of Western Art, as well as my parents.

For Felix Mayr-Harting

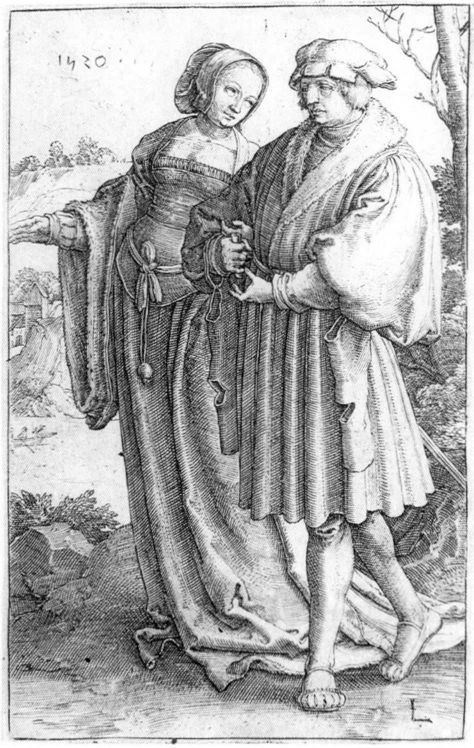

Ashmolean Museum, Eldon Gallery
8 July - 27 September, 1997

Above: Lucas van Leyden, *The Promenade*, 1520. 113:72 (borderlines) [cat. no. 50].
Front cover: Master FVB, *The Judgement of Solomon*. 263:217 (sheet) [cat. no. 34].
Back cover: Master W with the Key, *Interior of a Gothic Church*. 153:232 (borderlines) [cat. no. 21].

ISBN 1 85444 105 1

British Library Cataloguing-in-Publication data:
a catalogue record for this book is available from the British Library.

Designed and typeset in Bembo by Andrew Ivett.
Printed and bound in Great Britain by Cheney & Sons Ltd., Banbury.

CONTENTS

ABBREVIATIONS

H: Hollstein, F.W.H., *Dutch and Flemish Etchings, Engravings and Woodcuts*, ca. *1450-1700*, Amsterdam, 1949–.

NH: Filedt Kok, Jan Piet, *The New Hollstein Dutch & Flemish Etchings, Engravings and Woodcuts 1450-1700: Lucas van Leyden*, Ger Luijten (ed), Amsterdam, 1996.

L: Lehrs, Max, *Geschichte und kritischer Katalog des deutschen, niederländischen und französischen Kupferstichs im XV. Jahrhundert,* 9 vols, Vienna 1908-1934.

B: Bartsch, Adam, *Le Peintre-Graveur*, 21 vols, Paris, 1803-21.

dimensions: given in mm, height before width.

*Indicates that the work is illustrated in this catalogue.

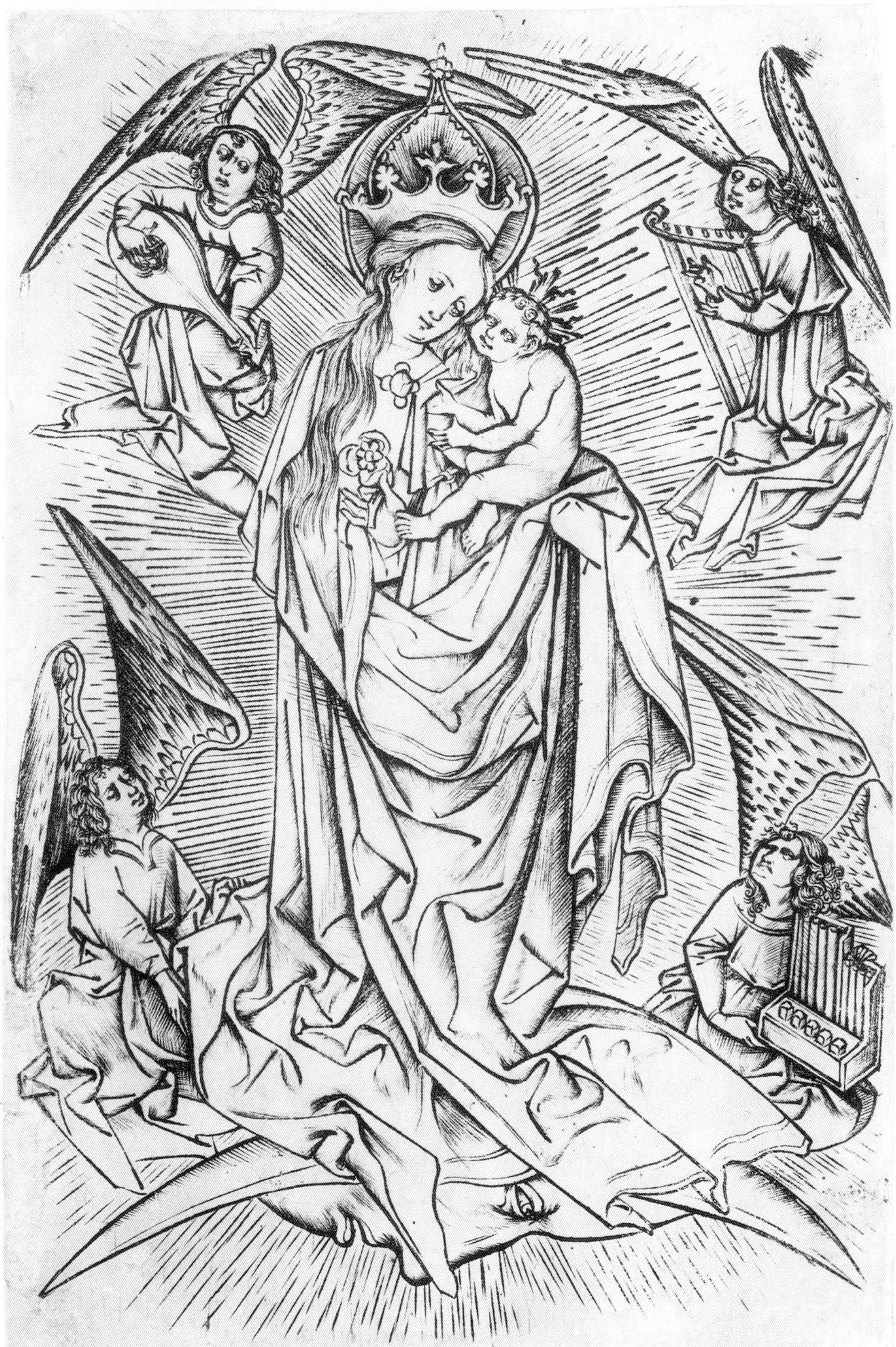

Master of the Death of the Virgin, *The Virgin and Child on a Crescent Moon, surrounded by four Angels*. 190:132 (borderlines) [cat. no. 1]. Actual size.

EARLY NETHERLANDISH ENGRAVING *c*. 1440-1540

The art of printing from engraved metal plates onto paper almost certainly began in the workshops of the Southern German goldsmiths during the 1430s. Engraving itself was not a new phenomenon since it had been widely practised for centuries by metal workers and jewellery makers. However, it was only in the early 15th century that the first paper mills were opened in Northern Europe, with paper becoming more widely available in the decades following Johannes Gutenberg's invention of movable type *c*.1440 and the printing industry that thus emerged. The increased supply of paper soon gave rise to the practice of lifting an impression from an engraved plate. This not only preserved the goldsmith-engraver's painstaking and intricate designs for future use in his workshop, but also gave an independent value to the printed image as a work of art itself.

Engravings were commonly made on plates of copper because the metal is relatively soft and good for cutting into with the burin. This is a sharp metal tool, shaped so that the greater the pressure applied, the deeper and wider the incision made, and consequently the more ink the line will hold. By engraving a variety of finely and deeply incised lines the full tonal range from light to shade may therefore be depicted. After a plate had been engraved it would be covered in ink and then wiped clean so that ink only remained in the cut lines. A slightly dampened sheet of paper was then placed on top of the plate and pressure applied from a press, so that the paper was forced into the grooves drawing the ink onto it. This type of printmaking is known as *intaglio* printing (*intagliare* means 'to cut into' in Italian). It is the opposite to printing from a woodcut, where the image is in *relief*. The pressure of the press during printing would gradually wear down the soft metal of the copper plate so there was a limited number of impressions that could be pulled, depending on how deeply the plate had been engraved and how carefully it had been treated in the press. The number of impressions made from a plate is very difficult to estimate, especially since they were probably printed as needed rather than all at once. What scarce documentary evidence there is suggests a plate was expected to produce several thousand prints before being completely exhausted (although only a small proportion would be of outstanding quality). Plates were often reworked with the burin, either by the original engraver or a later owner of the plate, so that they could be reprinted.

The earliest known engravers in the Netherlands were the Master of the Gardens of Love and, according to Lehrs, the Master of the Death of the Virgin[1], whose work dates from the late 1430s or early 1440s. As in Germany, the earliest masters (up to about the last quarter of the 15th century) were probably goldsmiths, after which the practice of engraving moved more into the realm of the painter's workshop. Engravings seem to have travelled very quickly from Germany down the Rhine to the Netherlands, for throughout the whole of the 15th century Netherlandish engravers remained indebted to the technical innovations of their German counterparts, such as the Master ES, Schongauer, and Dürer. It was only in the early 16th century, with the advent of Lucas van Leyden, that Netherlandish engravings began to gain anything like equal prestige as autonomous works of art with those of the great German masters, above all Albrecht Dürer, and to develop a distinctively Netherlandish conception of engraving.

The thriving art market of Northern Europe was well-suited to the rapid exchange of engravings over considerable distances, chiefly because there were obvious centres of art-production and exchange. In the Netherlands the market was concentrated in cities like Bruges, Ghent and Antwerp in the south and Utrecht in the north. Of these, Bruges was by far the most prominent with a huge turnover of foreign visitors and artists until about 1475, after which Antwerp took its place. Twice a year the Great Fairs, of Bruges in the Spring, and of Frankfurt in the Autumn, took place for about a month (both of these fairs already existed in the 13th century). People would travel great distances to come and buy and sell and thus the fairs provided a focal point for the exchange of paintings, artefacts and prints across Northern Europe, as well as being centres for the trade in paper. Engravings were also commonly sold directly from artists' workshops, at pilgrimage centres and by itinerant pedlars. Later in the century, as people first began to make collections of prints, dealers started to emerge such as the two who were members of the Bruges Guild of Illuminators, Pieter van Middembliic, *prentvercoopere*, (1481/2-1494) and Maertin van Axele, *de prenter coper*, (1490-1492)[2].

It is difficult to assess how much engravings cost in precise terms, especially since the surviving evidence about prices tends to date from the early 16th rather than the 15th century. In general, prints did not cost much and prices which were recorded, for instance the *goldgulden* [cat. nos. 63-64] which Lucas van Leyden received for one of his folio engravings (according to Karel van Mander[3]) were indicative of something exceptional rather than the norm. Dürer's diary of his journey to the Netherlands in 1521 shows that he sold one of his large and finely worked prints for less than the cost of a pair of shoes or of two dinners at an inn[4]. Although engravings were regarded more highly than woodcuts, at least before Dürer began designing woodcuts, they were cheap enough to have broad popular appeal, affordable to many artisans. Equally, it is likely that engravings were not particulary sought after by the wealthiest classes during the 15th century, who could afford more luxurious items such as paintings, tapestries and illuminated manuscripts. Yet, by the early 16th century the elite clearly saw the value, not least for political purposes, of commissioning and owning engravings, exemplified in the portrait engraving of the Habsburg Emperor and Regent in the Netherlands, *Maximilian I* by Lucas van Leyden [NH 172].

Engravings incorporated a wide range of subject matter from the sacred to the profane, from courtly love to violence and from the literary to the purely ornamental. It is the diversity of subject matter, particularly the inclusion of the chivalric theme of courtly love, which has led to the suggestion that engravings were intended for a slightly wealthier and more cosmopolitan clientele than single-leaf woodcuts. Woodcuts tended to be cruder artistically, devotional in theme, and from the 1460s, frequently made to illustrate books. Engravers had greater freedom both iconographically and stylistically than woodcut-designers since they were producing prints for the open market rather than for a monopolising source of patronage as book-illustration came to be for the production of woodcuts. It was not until 1476 that engravings were first specifically designed as illustrations for a book. Commissioned by Colard Mansion for his French translation of Boccaccio's book on the unfortunate figures of myth and history, *De la Ruine des nobles Hommes et Femmes*, published in Bruges in 1476, they show an important transition in the type of illustration desired for books. However, the project was never fully accomplished, perhaps on account of the impracticality of combining two methods of printing: relief printing for the text and intaglio printing for the illustrations. The engravings are pasted into the three surviving copies of the book[5].

Given the creative freedom that the open-market brought to engravers, it was natural that they should look for inspiration to the great strengths of Netherlandish art, in particular panel painting and miniature painting in illuminated manuscripts. Many 15th-century engravings, particularly those of a religious nature, probably reproduced paintings or miniatures in illuminated manuscripts (now generally lost). These were not 'reproductions' in the strict sense of the word, for the engraver's copying meant adapting a successful prototype rather than translat-

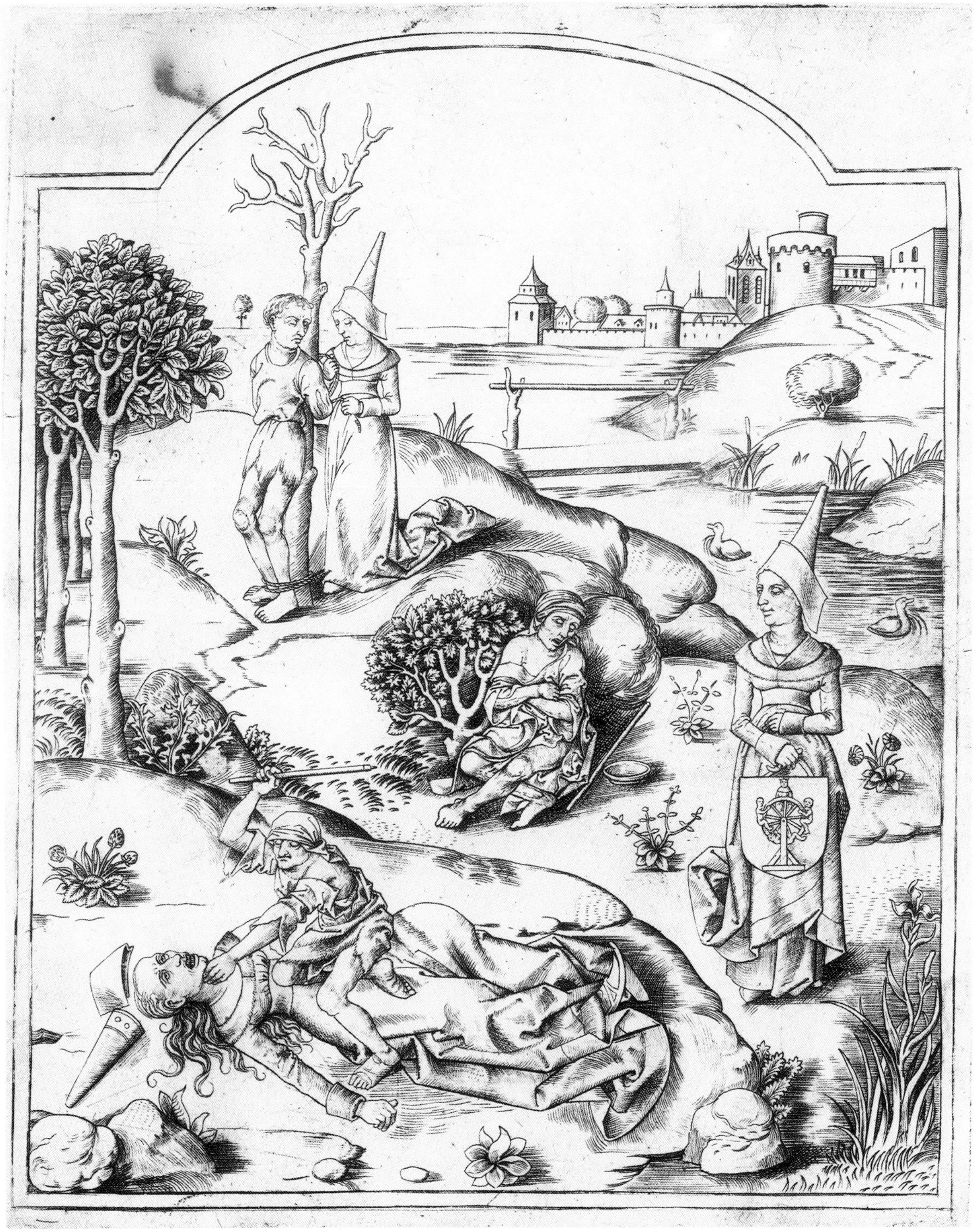

Master of the Boccaccio Illustrations, *The Fight of Fortune with Poverty*. 213:175 (platemark) [cat. no. 12].

ing the individual style of a painter into a graphic medium, which only began in earnest from the mid-16th century onwards.

It may be argued that the very strength of the Netherlandish tradition of painting, which remained unrivalled across Northern Europe in the 15th century, was a factor which inhibited the early progress of engraving and helps to explain why Netherlandish engravers did not develop the sophisticated technique of their German contemporaries until the 16th century. It was during this period that Jan van Eyck was producing his 'jewel-like' oil paintings on panel, the first of a succession of great Southern Netherlandish painters, which included Rogier van der Weyden, Petrus Christus, Hans Memling and Dieric Bouts, working for the Court of the Dukes of Burgundy, other European courts, foreign merchants or the wealthy middle classes of Bruges and elsewhere. However, none of these great painters ventured into engraving themselves and enriched it with their skilled draughtsmanship, as Martin Schongauer and Albrecht Dürer did in Germany, or Andrea Mantegna in Italy.

Secondly, engraving had begun to emerge in the Netherlands about 1440, just as the city of Bruges entered its period of exceptional prosperity *c.* 1440-1475. It is possible that the booming economy of Bruges during these years meant that there was less demand for images in a medium of inferior status among those who might most have been expected to stimulate demand, namely the middle classes of the city. It seems that while the prosperity of these citizens lasted they preferred to commission paintings or at least to buy copies painted in the workshop rather than to buy engravings. Apart from the obvious enjoyment of owning a painting, it was a means of enhancing their social status by emulating the patronage of the elite[6]. Although the two phenomena are not directly related, it is interesting to note that at just about the same time as the extraordinary prosperity of Bruges collapsed, engraving in the Netherlands began to be much more widely practised by artists such as Master FVB, Master W with the Key and Master IAM of Zwolle and to develop much more rapidly in terms of technique. Moreover, it was in the final quarter of the 15th century that these engravers began to sign their plates with monograms to establish their authorship, a good indication that the value of engravings as works of art was increasing.

Thirdly, the quintessence of Netherlandish painting was the notion of light illuminating the viewer's perception of the colour and the texture of the things before it. Consequently, 15th-century panels are full of rich, luminous colour and appear 'realistic' in the way even the most minute reflections of light are observed, from a metal stud on a shoe to the refractions of light in a glass. Translating these ideas into a black and white, linear mode was far from straightforward. It required complex systems of hatching which were well beyond the skill of the earliest engravers. Until solutions to this problem could be found, there is a sense in which engraving as a medium was unable to fulfill the particular Netherlandish aesthetic of light as a means of representation. Master FVB began to develop a more tonal approach under the influence of Schongauer, but it was only in the engravings of Lucas van Leyden at the beginning of the 16th century that a truly painterly method of engraving was found. His colouristic notion of engraving was in keeping with the great Netherlandish tradition of painting, seeking to overcome the essential linear quality of the medium by using minutely varied systems of hatching which could portray the subtle middle-tones of colour and achieve a sense of light diffused throughout the image. While deeply indebted to Dürer, Lucas van Leyden produced quite different results from his essentially graphic designs, in which the colour of the paper was as much part of Dürer's conception of an engraving as the rich black ink in which it was printed[7].

Prints of all types of subject matter were useful as a means of transmitting ideas among artists and craftsmen working in different media.

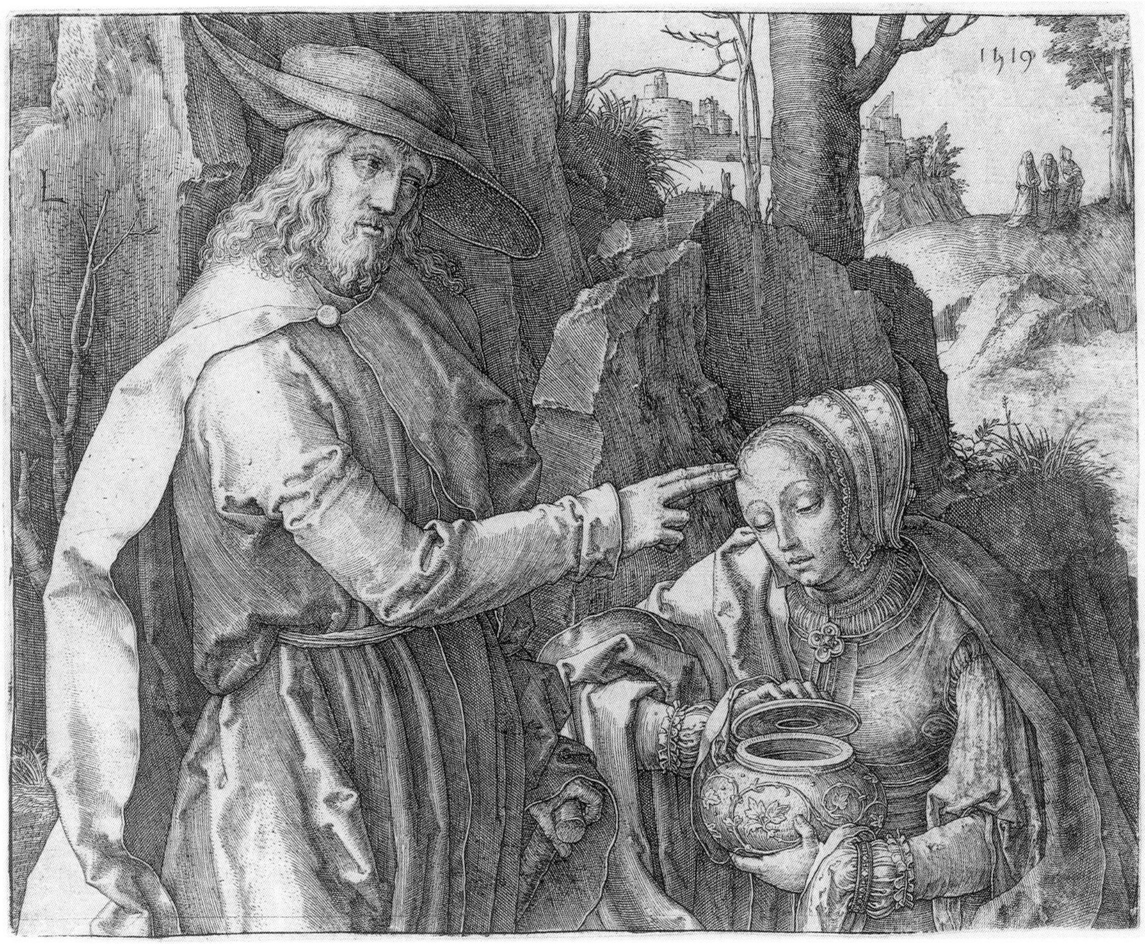

Lucas van Leyden, *Christ appearing to Mary Magdalen as a Gardener*, 1519. 132:167 (borderlines) [cat. no. 48].

Engravers often borrowed motifs and compositions from each other (consider Master FVB's copy of Schongauer's *Ornament with an Owl* [cat. no. 35] and the relation of his *Judgement of Solomon* [cat. no. 34] to that of the Master ES [L, II, 7]) and from other media (such as the influence of Rogier van der Weyden on the early work of Master IAM of Zwolle and Dieric Bouts on Master FVB). In turn, engravings were also used as models for manuscript illuminations (for example the Master of the Berlin Passion's *Ornament with a Couple playing Chess* [cat no. 2]), sculpture in wood and alabaster (perhaps Master IAM of Zwolle's *Last Supper* and *Arrest of Christ* [cat. nos. 31-32]), precious metalwork (Master W with the Key's *Censer*, *Crosier* and *Monstrance* [cat. nos. 16-18]), glass painting (Dirck Vellert's *Vision of St Bernard* [cat no. 42]), ivory work, tiles, embroidery, leather work, as well as for paintings.

Many 15th- and early 16th-century paintings depict engravings pinned to walls, pasted to chairs, stuck around fireplaces, pinned above beds or stuck on doorposts and trees during festivals. The meaning invested in engravings displayed in this way depended both on the subject matter (an ornamental print would have had a purely decorative function, whereas there might have been more complex motives for putting up a sacred or profane image), the location in which the householder chose to place it (there would have been different reasons

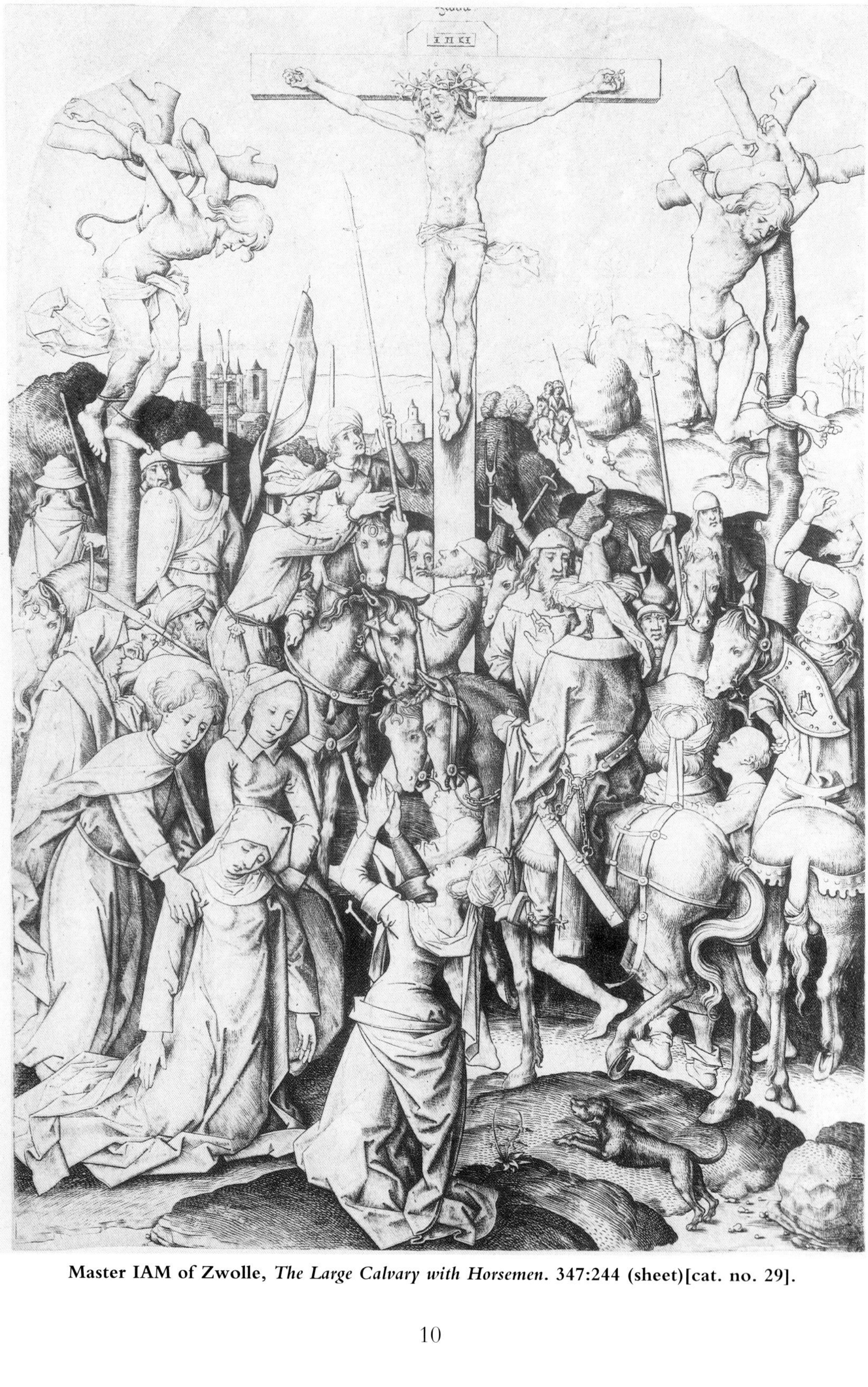

Master IAM of Zwolle, *The Large Calvary with Horsemen*. **347:244 (sheet)[cat. no. 29].**

behind placing an engraving in a public or private part of the house), and whom they thought likely to see the engravings.

Religious engravings put up in the home were no doubt intended to inspire godly living among the family themselves, often being used in less wealthy homes in the place of panel paintings to set up make-shift altars where votive offerings could be made. These would probably have been the larger and more finely worked prints, such as the engraving of *The Large Calvary with Horsemen* by Master IAM of Zwolle [cat. no. 29]. The underlying sense that God himself was watching meant that engravings acquired a kind of talismanic significance as outward signs of inward devotion, which it was hoped would bring God's protection and blessing to the household. Visitors to the home gave engravings a public meaning, expressing the household's participation in a society which greatly valued private devotion. These reasons may help to explain the widespread popularity of scenes of the Annunciation taking place in the Virgin's bedroom, since this was surely one of the most profound religious experiences of a woman within her own home.

One of the most common uses of religious engravings was as an aid to private prayer. Monasteries often produced their own prints 'in house', in order to supply their community with an image such as the Crucifixion or a patron saint on which they could meditate as they prayed through the daily office. Monasteries situated at centres of pilgrimage also produced woodcuts, and on occasions engravings, to be sold to pilgrims as religious mementoes (and sometimes as indulgences) of both spiritual and touristic significance. The practice, common among pilgrims, of wearing engravings pinned to hats or clothing may be seen in the engraving *Pilgrims*, 1508 by Lucas van Leyden [cat. no. 46].

Prayer was a central feature of life for laymen and women as well as for the clergy. Those wealthy enough often chose to commission a beautifully illuminated Book of Hours. To own such a lavish book was a means of conspicuous devotion which asserted earthly status as well as spiritual elevation above the generality. The long-standing tradition of miniature painting in the Netherlands is central to understanding one of the most important functions of engravings for the middle classes in the 15th century. Unable to afford their own illuminated Book of Hours, they acquired engravings to paste into prayer books as a means of copying the practice of the elite. There was, therefore, a huge market for devotional prints, which would often be hand-painted before being pasted into a prayer book to make them look more like illuminated miniatures. The unique series of *The Passion* [cat. nos. 3-10] by the Master of the Boccaccio Illustrations is a prime example.

However, prints were not simply the poor relation of illuminated manuscripts. A Book of Hours in the British Library, probably from the Lower Rhenish region of Limbourg *c.* 1463-76, uses a number of prints by the Master of the Berlin Passion, including *Ornament with a Couple playing Chess* [cat. no. 2], as models for the miniatures and the decorative borders around the text[8]. It is an unusually clear example of how early in the 15th century engraving began to influence illumination. The sustained borrowing between engraving, illumination and panel painting over a number of decades resulted in the use of generic types of representation which may be observed in a comparison of the late 15th-century engraving of *The Annunciation* by the Bruges Master FVB [cat. no. 33] and a folio illustration of the same scene in an early 16th-century Book of Hours, also probably from Bruges, painted by the Master of the David Scenes in the Grimani Breviary [cat. no. 60], both of which appear to be derived from a painting by Rogier van der Weyden now in Munich[9]. It is also worth noting that the two printsellers of Bruges, mentioned above, were part of the Guild of Illuminators rather than the painters' Guild of St Luke, showing the close alliance which existed between engravings and manuscripts.

Besides the whole tradition of Christian morality, engravers drew on a wealth of secular, moralistic stories and proverbs, often concerned with issues of temperance and sexual continence, which were popular in the Netherlands at the time. Behind the moral point of scenes like *Two Peasants quarrelling over a Game of Skittles* by Master FVB [cat. no. 37] or *Virgil suspended in a Basket* by Lucas van Leyden [cat. no. 51] was a type of Northern European humour, laughing at the ridiculous situations into which man's folly leads him, particularly when confronted with the alluring delights of women. Such humour could reach biting extremes, especially when combined with other strands of contemporary thought such as the anticlericalism present in the lustful attack of the *Monk and the Woman Spinning* by the Master FVB [cat. no. 38]. The small size of an engraving like this gave it a confidential, 'hide-able' quality, leaving the engraver with a sense of freedom to depict subjects in the sort of intimate and graphic detail which painters, apart from Hieronymus Bosch, tended to find unsuitable. A more optimistic note of romance is to be found in the *Ornament with a Couple playing Chess* by the Master of the Berlin Passion [cat no. 2], in which the game of chess points to the often complex game of winning love, or Lucas van Leyden's engraving of *The Promenade*, 1520 [cat. no. 50] which depicts the pleasure of husband and wife walking by a river. This is, as it were, a close-up adapted from an extremely popular subject in Netherlandish paintings and prints of the 15th century, namely the Garden of Love, in which couples were portrayed enjoying the delights of love amid the cultivated beauty of nature. Derived from medieval ideas about courtly love, engravings of this theme would have had a particular appeal among the more educated, as well as being attractive and light-hearted images in themselves.

By the early 16th century engraving had begun to be considered as a medium which had its own intrinsic aesthetic value in making works of art, chiefly due to the ubiquitous acclaim given to Dürer. In 1609 Mathias Quadt von Kinkelbach, a German, wrote a travellers' guide to his country, which included the first substantial history of printmaking in Germany and the Netherlands[10]. Master FVB was the earliest Netherlandish engraver he discussed, suggesting that it was with this master that Netherlandish engravings began to gain a status for what they were as works of art, rather than for what their use might be. It is only at this stage that one may reasonably call any Netherlander a 'painter-engraver' (to use the term coined by Adam Bartsch in 1803[11]) and in comparison to the artistic quality of German and Italian painter-engravers working at the end of the 15th century, it is a term most securely applied first to Lucas van Leyden in the early 16th century. He was the first Netherlandish artist to see the opportunity for personal renown in producing engravings which were refined, autonomous works. His engravings were already much sought after by collectors during his lifetime and the wide range of biblical, classical, medieval and popular sources he used show he was chiefly producing prints for an erudite clientele. However, it had become an art market dominated by connoisseurs, for whom the quality of the master's hand in an engraving, rather than the subject depicted, had become the most important criterion for its desirability.

Of equal importance to Lucas van Leyden for the stylistic development of Netherlandish engraving during the 16th century was the contribution of the painter Jan Gossaert, who made just one etching, two engravings and two woodcuts in contrast to Lucas's prolific output. Gossaert's style was deeply affected by his discovery of antique sculpture and the Italian Renaissance when he stayed in Rome from 1507 to 1508 in the retinue of Philip of Burgundy, an illegitimate son of Philip the Handsome, Duke of Burgundy from 1482-1506. As a result he was credited by Karel van Mander as having introduced classical ideals of beauty into Netherlandish art and, therefore, to have laid the basis for the Mannerist painters and engravers such as Van Mander himself, Hendrick Goltzius and

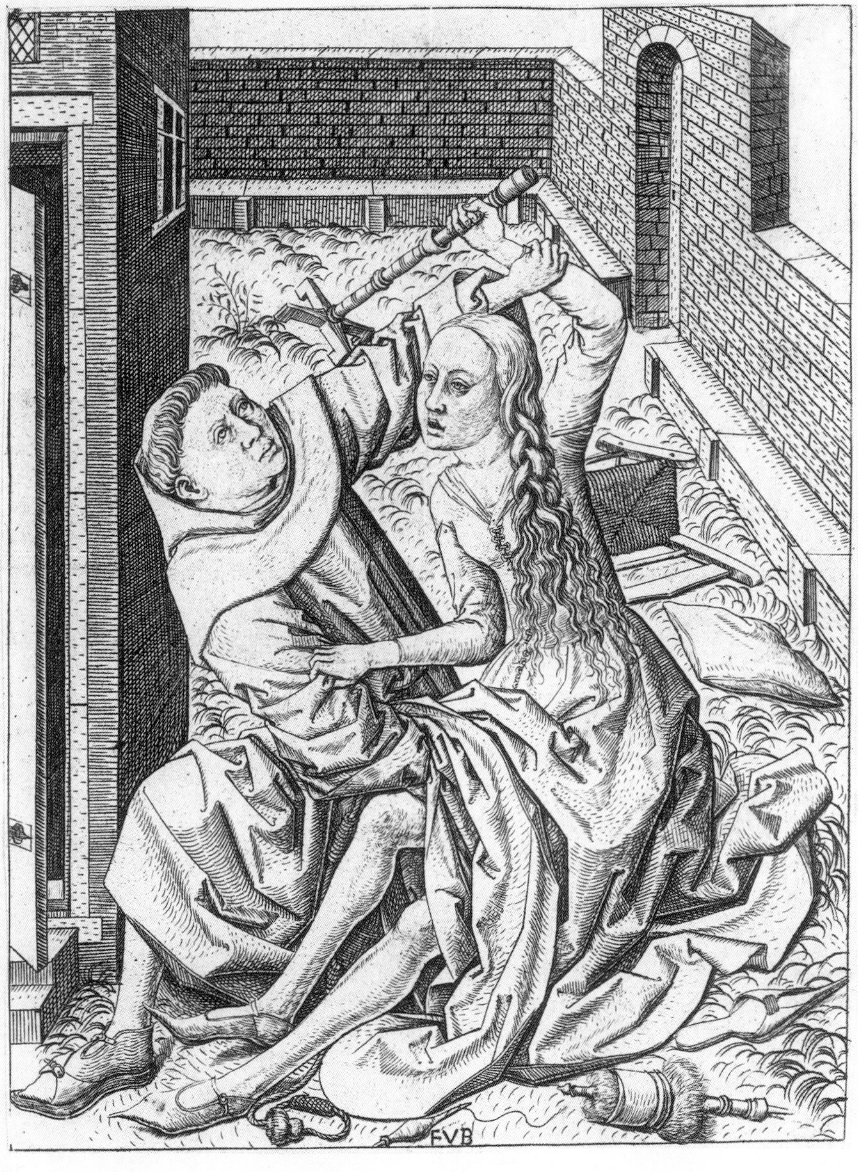

Master FVB, *The Monk and the Woman Spinning*. 158:120 (borderlines) [cat. no. 38]. Actual size.

Abraham Bloemart, whose style dominated later 16th-century engraving. These ideals had also been seen in the prints of Marcantonio Raimondi which filtered north through Gossaert and others in the first third of the 16th century. The impact of Marcantonio's monumental treatment of the human figure and his use of bold cross-hatching is manifest not only in Gossaert's work but also that of Lucas van Leyden, Frans Crabbe van Espleghem and Dirck Vellert among others.

All the engravings in this exhibition previously belonged to one of two owners, the Reverend F. W. Hope and Mr Francis Douce. Hope founded the Chair of Entomology at Oxford University and was its first Professor (the Chair still bears his name). The group of four

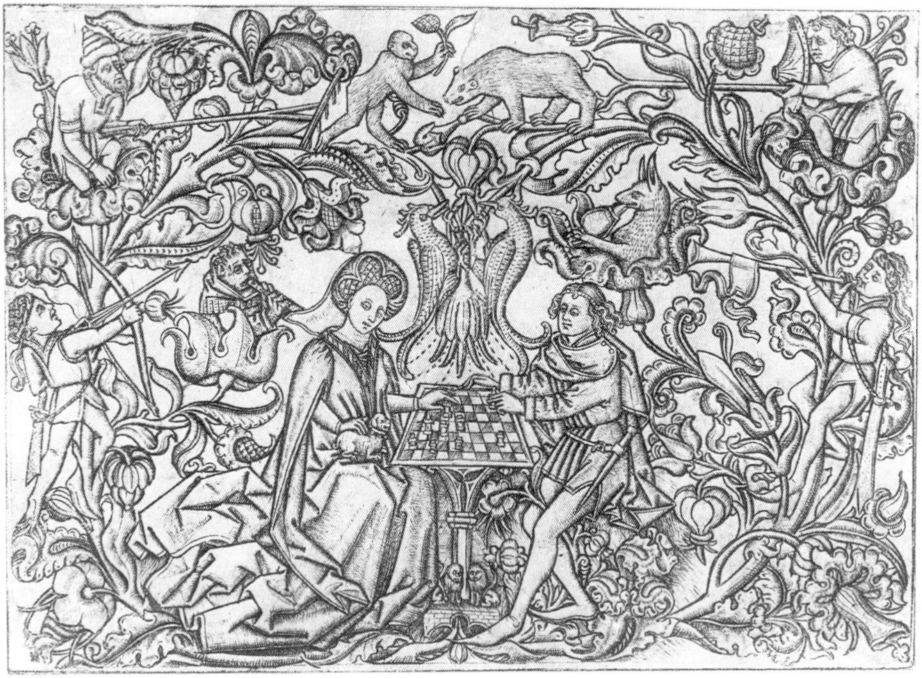

Master of the Berlin Passion, *Ornament with a Couple playing Chess*. 105:145 (borderlines) [cat. no. 2].

engravings by Master W with the Key was an exceptional element in his collection of tens of thousands of prints, mostly portraits dating from the 16th to the 19th centuries, which he presented to Oxford University in 1850. Francis Douce bequeathed his vast collection of illuminated manuscripts, antiquarian books, prints and drawings to the University in 1834. After the death of his father he had been able to live by modest private means, becoming a collector and connoisseur in a number of fields. Douce acquired early European engravings from the start of his collecting career, either buying or exchanging them with London dealers (and friends) like Samuel Woodburn, Thomas Rodd, Triphook and Thomas Dodd. Late in life he inherited considerable wealth from the sculptor Joseph Nollekens and was able to purchase exceptional treasures, for example the illuminated Book of Hours by the Master of Mary of Burgundy, now in the Bodleian Library. Douce kept a diary of the purchases he had made each month for about thirty years[12]. Many of the references to his acquisition of prints in this diary are very vague. However, he described those that particularly caught his attention. For instance,

July 1808, "Some lots of old Masters at Allen's sale by Dodd, among which was a most curious print by Zwoll and many that I never saw before",

May 1813, "A parcel of prints miscell. of Baldwin among which was L. Van Leyden's Magdalen",

August 1829, "Boccaccio. anc. cuts. Rodd".

Much of Douce's success as a collector must have been based on a sort of archaelogical instinct about early prints and a good eye since he was sailing in waters which were largely uncharted in reference books. Douce's print collection in the Ashmolean is one of the major collections which has provided future generations with the means of research fundamental to our understanding of the first century of printmaking.

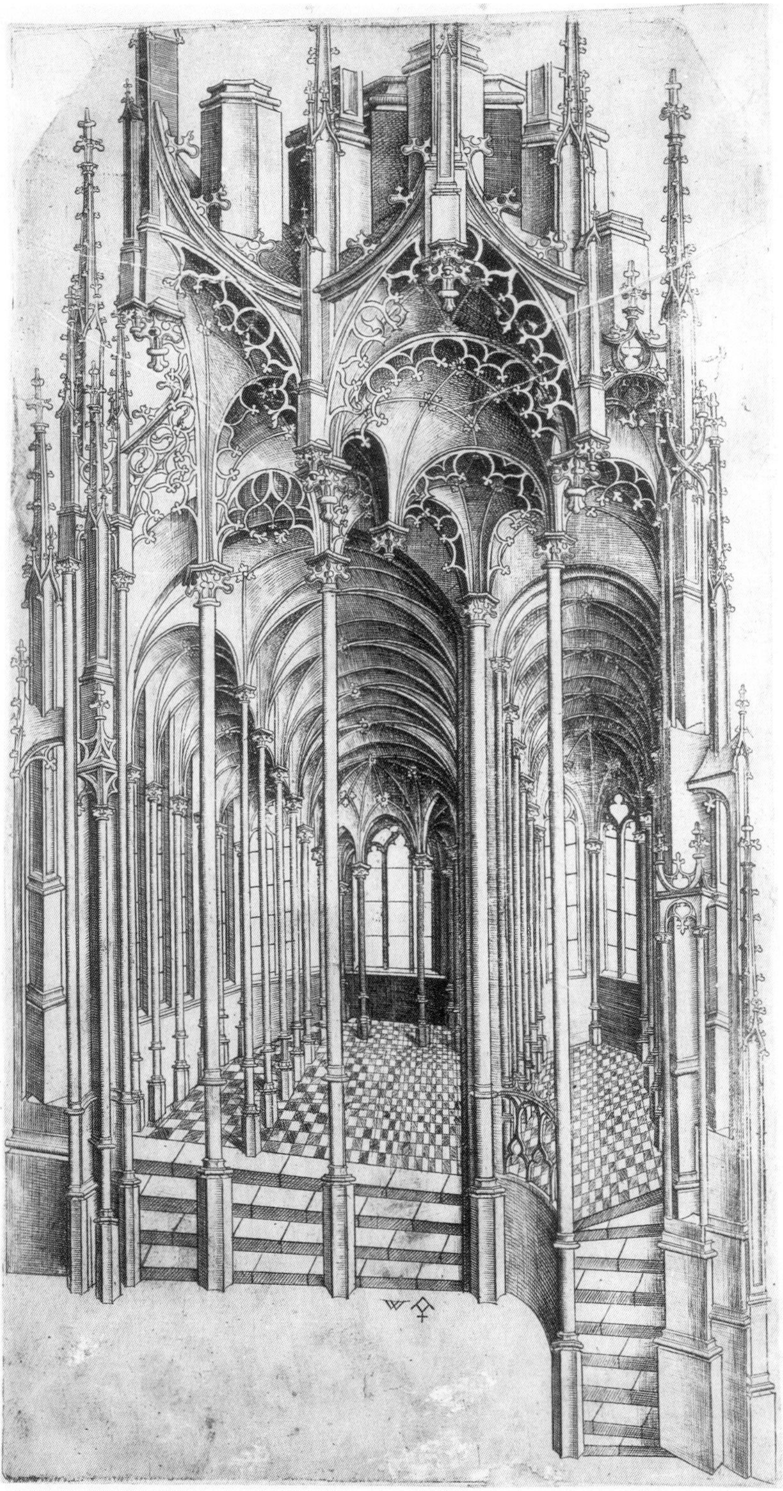

Master W with the Key, *Interior of a Gothic Hall*. 346:190 (platemark) [cat. no. 22].

CATALOGUE

EARLY NETHERLANDISH ENGRAVING, *c.* 1440-1540

Master of the Death of the Virgin (*fl c.* 1440)

This master, perhaps from the Southern Netherlands[13], was one of the first goldsmiths to use his engraving for printing on paper. Although the various techniques of the earliest engravers were determined partly by the differing tools they used, the Master's strong outlines followed by short, light strokes for the areas of shading are characteristic features of this period.

(1)★ *The Virgin and Child on a Crescent Moon surrounded by four Angels*
Engraving; 190:132 (borderlines)
Hollstein, XII, p. 195; Lehrs, I, 3
Bequeathed by Francis Douce, 1834

This is a very fine early impression, in which some of the broadest lines appear blurred at the edges, perhaps caused by unsophisticated early printing methods. The handling of the faces, other than that of the Virgin, and the foreshortening of the angels' wings is rather crude.

Master of the Berlin Passion (*fl c.* 1450-70)

The Master of the Berlin Passion, so-called because seven of his engravings of *The Passion* are pasted into a prayer book now in Berlin, was one of the most important of second-generation Netherlandish engravers. His skill as a goldsmith is evident in the intricate decoration of his ornamental works, among the earliest of their kind. His use of cross-hatching to model form was extremely delicate and shows the influence of his contemporary, the German Master ES. Max Geisberg identified the Master as Israhel van Meckenem the elder active in Bocholt[14]. He and the younger Israhel van Meckenem used the same housemark to sign some of their plates (a privilege confined to the eldest son of a master), and the younger Israhel is believed to have reworked the plates of the Master of the Berlin Passion (he also reworked plates by Master ES and Master FVB). The miniatures and decorative borders in a Book of Hours from Limbourg, now in the British Library[15], show a particularly close connection with the Master's engravings, but this does not seem ground enough on which to suggest Limbourg was his centre of activity. Yet it does show that the one hundred and nineteen engravings attributed to the Master were influential in the region of the Lower Rhine and are known to have been copied not only by this miniaturist but also by other engravers.

(2)★ *Ornament with the Couple playing Chess*
Engraving, 105:145 (borderlines)
Hollstein, XII, p. 111; Lehrs, III, 115
Bequeathed by Francis Douce, 1834

This is a unique impression of one of the Master of the Berlin Passion's most attractive ornamental engravings. The woman's power in the game of love, a popular theme in 15th-century engravings, is evident in the contrast of the young knight playing chess against a lady of obviously greater standing, with her elegant headdress and small dog on her lap. Their incompatability is amusingly echoed in the monkey and bear being pushed together above them.

Master of the Boccaccio Illustrations (*fl* 1476)

The anonymous engraver of nine illustrations to a French translation of Boccaccio, *De la Ruine des nobles Hommes et Femmes* (published by Colard Mansion in Bruges in 1476) was given the name Master of the Boccaccio Illustrations in the mid-19th century. Other engravings such as the series of *The Passion* have also been attributed to this artist, who appears to have have been active around the Burgundian Court in the Southern Netherlands. Anzelwsky[16] established that the nine illustrations are the work of more than one master, some of which can be attributed to an engraver close in style to the Bruges illuminator known as the Master of the Dresden Prayerbook. His workshop was one of the most productive in the Netherlands producing about forty surviving manuscripts. The Master of the Dresden Prayerbook was one of the first miniaturists to capture differing moods and emotions, a quality evident in the engravings illustrating Boccaccio.

From a Series of *The Passion*:
(3) *Christ before Annas* 70:55 (borderlines)
(4) *Christ crowned with Thorns* 69:48 (borderlines)
(5) *Christ on the Cross with the Soldiers casting Lots below* 75:53 (borderlines)
(6) *Christ on the Cross and the repentant Thief* 74:54 (borderlines)
(7) *Christ on the Cross scoffed at by the Chief Priests* 74:54 (borderlines)
(8) *Christ on the Cross commends St John to his Mother* 73:50 (borderlines)
(9) *Christ on the Cross with the converted Centurion* 74:54 (borderlines)
(10) *Christ on the Cross speaking his last Words* 73:54 (borderlines)
Engravings, with bodycolour and gold leaf
Hollstein, XII, p. 116; Lehrs, IV, 12, 13, 15, 16, 17, 19, 20, 21
Bequeathed by Francis Douce, 1834

These prints are simply engraved, since they were probably intended to be coloured straightaway. The coloured frames and gilt edging with text beneath show that they would have been pasted into a prayer book as quasi-illuminated miniatures. The Italianate column-borders on some of the sheets are woodcuts of the type often used in printed books, which have been coloured and stuck down.

(11) *The Death of King Saul* (Book 2, Chapter 1)
Engraving; 202:165 (borderlines)
Hollstein, XII, p. 119; Lehrs, IV, 4 (ii)
Bequeathed by Francis Douce, 1834

The soldier in the left foreground is resheathing his sword while King Saul now lies dead. The artist has attempted to use shading lines around the figure of Saul to give the impression he is lying on the ground, but the King still appears to be floating.

(12)* *The Fight of Fortune with Poverty* (Book 3, Chapter 1)
Engraving; 213:175 (platemark)
Hollstein, XII, p. 120; Lehrs, IV, 5
Bequeathed by Francis Douce, 1834

Fortune (not so fat here as Boccaccio's narrative suggests) finds herself the worse off in her dispute with Poverty. The engraver captures the tense mood of conflict in the faces of the characters.

(13) *The Death of Regulus* (Book 5, Chapter 3)
Engraving; 194:161 (borderlines)
Hollstein, XII, p. 121; Lehrs, IV, 7
Bequeathed by Francis Douce, 1834

Marcus Atilius Regulus, the Roman consul in 256 BC, was captured in Tunis during the invasions of the first Punic War. He was allowed to return to Rome on parole to negotiate peace terms involving the exchange of prisoners. A posthumous tradition grew up that on his return he was subjected to the torture and execution depicted here.

(14) *The Execution of Queen Brunhilda* (Book 9, Chapter 1)
Engraving; 188:160 (borderlines)
Hollstein, XII, p. 122; Lehrs, IV, 10
Bequeathed by Francis Douce, 1834

It is alleged that Brunhilda, a Visigothic Queen of the 6th century living in exile in Burgundy, was executed by being dragged to death by wild horses after she had tried to claim Burgundy and Austrasia in the name of her great-grandson.

Master W with the Key (? Willem vanden Cruce) (*fl c.* 1465–90)

About eighty engravings are known by the artist who signed his plates with a *W* followed by his housemark. However, only one or two impressions of most of his plates survive, meaning that this is a remarkable group of his engravings. As one of the first Netherlandish engravers to denote his authorship by using a monogram, he was departing from the traditional anonymity of medieval craftsman and pointing to his own status as an artist. It is generally believed the Master had contacts with the Burgundian Court in Bruges since one of his engavings depicts the coat of arms of Charles the Bold, Duke of Burgundy [L, VII, 48] and he also made a series of engravings of the Burgundian army. A recent article suggests that the engraver could be the Bruges goldsmith Willem vanden Cruce and that thus his housemark should be read as an *A* over a cross (the Latinized form of vanden Cruce is *a Cruce*), rather than as a stylized key[17]. The Master's engravings indicate he ran a successful workshop supplying goldsmiths, shrinemakers and masons with designs (he may have practised one of these crafts himself). Some of these designs, like the *Large Crosier* [cat. no. 17], were unusually large and had to be made up of two plates, printed on separate sheets of paper which were then stuck together. The linear precision of engraving meant it was an ideal medium for the labyrinthine detail of the Master's Late Gothic style. Unlike many of the late 15th-, early 16th-century Netherlandish painter-engravers, Master W with the Key makes a virtue of strong graphic contrasts.

(15) *Gothic Altar with Eight Niches*
Engraving; 316:250 (borderlines), cut off at corners
At upper sides, under butresses: *W* and housemark
Hollstein, XII, p. 238; Lehrs, VII, 61
Presented by the Revd F. W. Hope, 1850

Statues of saints were probably intended to stand in the niches of the altar. To Max Lehrs this was the most important engraving for placing Master W with the Key in the locality of Bruges, on the grounds that altars such as this were rarely found anywhere else in the Netherlands.

(16)* *A Gothic Censer*
Engraving; 281:135 (borderlines)
At upper sides of censer: *W* and housemark
Hollstein, XII, p. 234; Lehrs, VII, 57
Bequeathed by Francis Douce, 1834

The use of a variety of different strokes suggests the reflection of light on the metal object. However, the purpose of the artist in so doing is to accentuate the ornate design, rather than to depict the fall of light with complete accuracy.

(17) *The Large Crosier* (lower plate)
Engraving; 328:119 (borderlines)
Hollstein, XII, p. 226; Lehrs, VII, 49 ([b], not [a] as in Lehrs)
Presented by the Revd F. W. Hope, 1850

This is the lower half of a bishop's crosier. The engraving was Master W with the Key's largest work, with a total height of almost 70 cms, suggesting it was a life-size model. This is one of two known impressions of the lower plate and there is a unique impression of the upper section in Vienna.

(18) A Gothic Monstrance (2 plates)
Engraving; 267:100 (borderlines of upper plate); 222:108 (borderlines of lower plate)
At upper sides of monstrance: *W* and housemark
Hollstein, XII, p. 232; Lehrs, VII, 55 (ii)
Bequeathed by Francis Douce, 1834

This design for a monstrance, in which the host or a relic might be displayed, is made up of two plates like *The Large Crosier* [cat. no. 17]. It is the only print by Master W with the Key to include the detail of a cross-section for the aid of the goldsmith.

(19) *Interior of a Gothic Chapel*
Engraving; 386:171 (borderlines)
At sides of canopy: *W* and housemark
Hollstein, XII, p. 243; Lehrs, VII, 66
Presented by the Revd. F. W. Hope, 1850

The canopies and borders which surround Master W with the Key's engravings of interiors suggest they may have been designs for tabernacles and shrines rather than real architectural features.

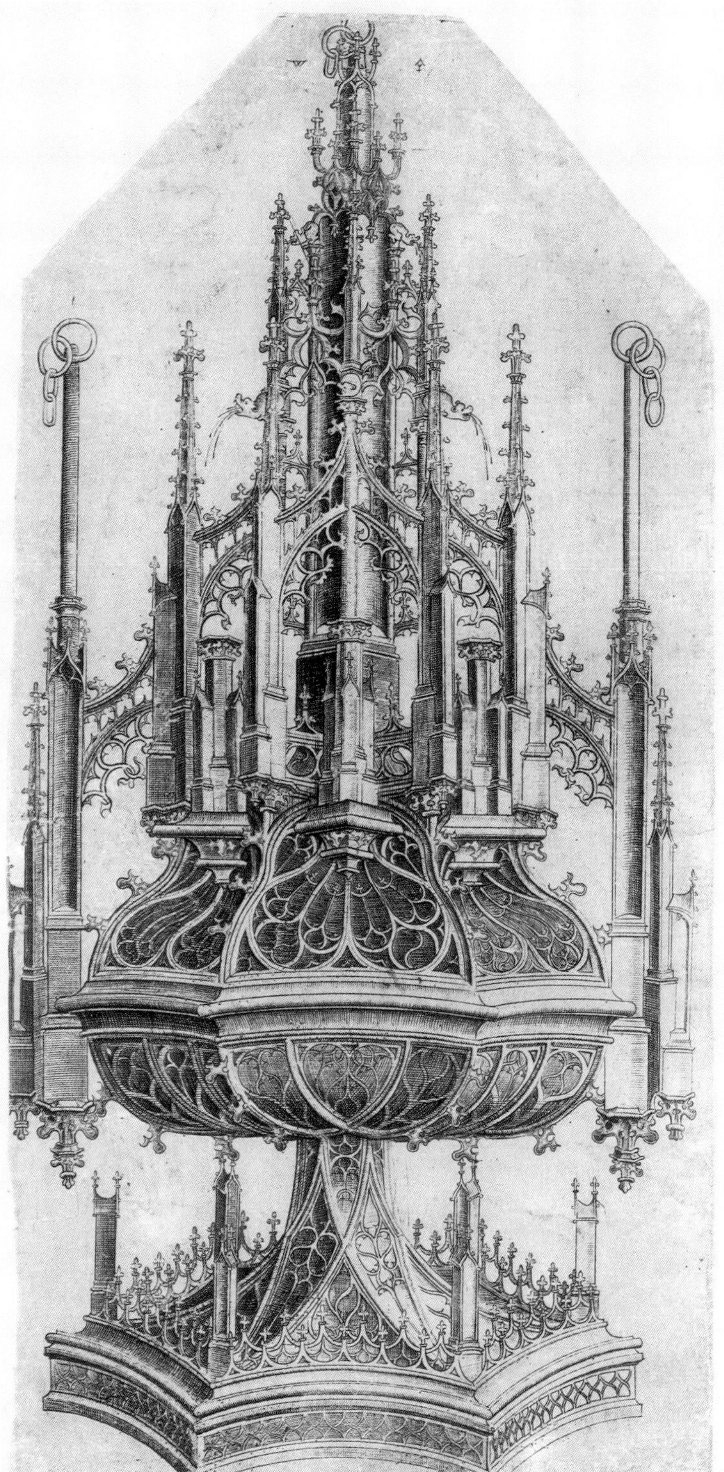

Master W with the Key, *A Gothic Censer.* 281:135 (borderlines) [cat. no. 16].

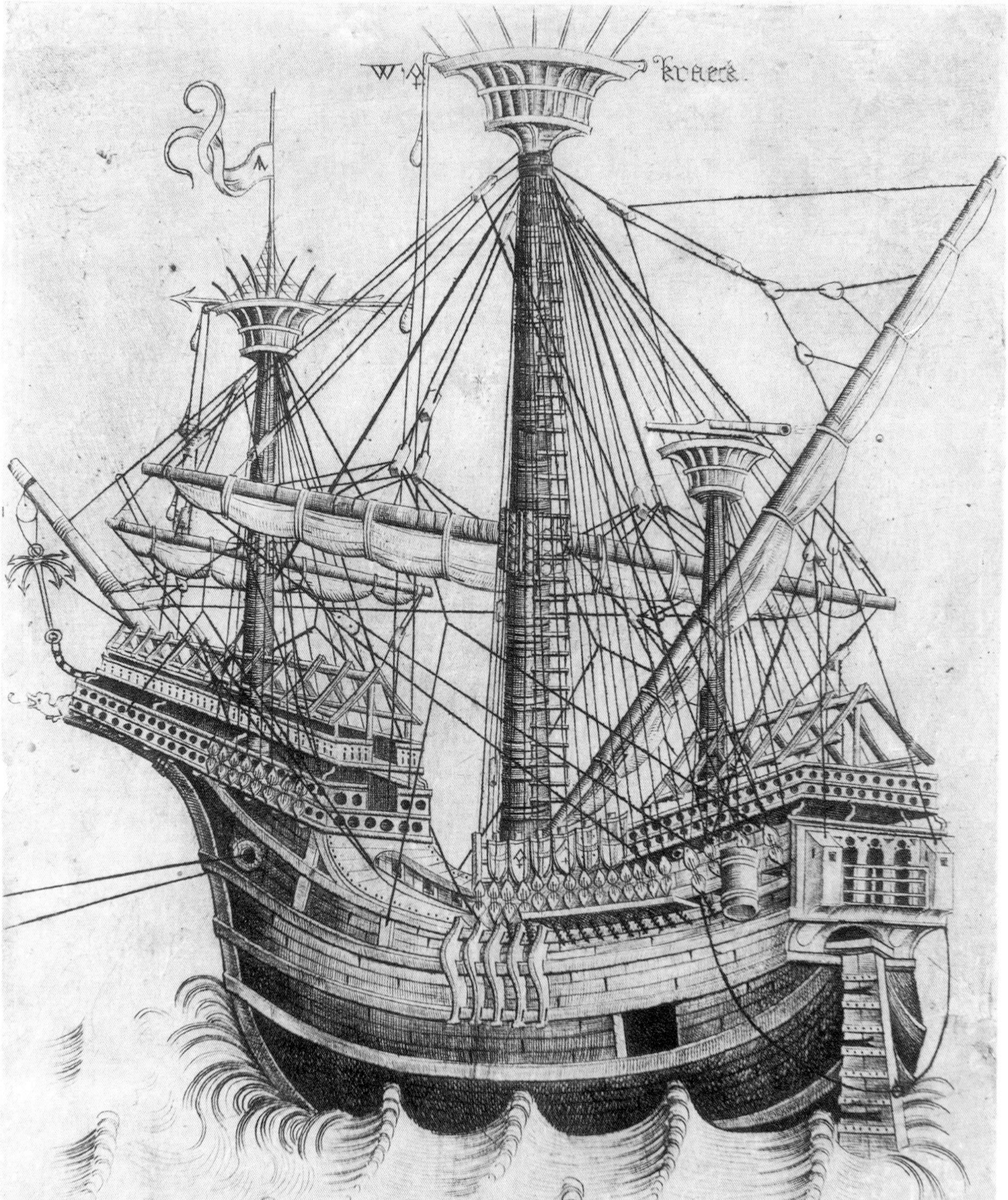

Master W with the Key, ***Man-of-War Ship, "kraeck".*** **200:157 (borderlines) [cat. no. 23]. Actual size.**

(20) *Vista through the Interior of a Chapel*
Engraving; 225:111 (platemark)
At sides of centre pinnacle: *W* and housemark
Hollstein, XII, p. 241; Lehrs, VII, 64
Bequeathed by Francis Douce, 1834

The vista seen through the windows of the gothic chapel makes it clear that this interior is to be understood as an architectural feature rather than a small shrine. The light falling through the windows from the right is echoed in the fine strokes of the burin on the land and in the trees, giving the impression of sunshine.

(21)* *Interior of a Gothic Church*
Engraving; 153:132 (borderlines)
Hollstein, XII, p. 240; Lehrs, VII, 63 (i)
Bequeathed by Francis Douce, 1834

The eye of the viewer is unable to rest since the vanishing point of the interior lies hidden directly behind the row of pillars (towards the base) which support the right side of the central aisle. The space appears as an expanse unlimited by the eye, since the side walls stop short of the far end, opening into bays at the left and right which one cannot see.

(22)* *Interior of a Gothic Hall*
Engraving; 346:190 (platemark)
Below steps: *W* and housemark
Hollstein, XII, p. 242; Lehrs, VII, 65
Presented by the Revd F. W. Hope, 1850

The 'realistic' perspective is an illusion, since the two sections of the hall have their own vanishing point (the point at which all the lines of perspective converge). The mishandling of the perspective of the steps, particularly at the right, leaves one dizzy, as if the floor were on a slope in the foreground but level at the far end.

(23)* *Man-of-War Ship turned to left, "kraeck"*
Engraving; 200:157 (borderlines)
At sides of mast: *W* and housemark and *kraeck*; on a shield at base of mast: housemark.
Hollstein, XII, p. 220; Lehrs, VII, 41
Bequeathed by Francis Douce, 1834

This ship is the most spectacular of the Master's series of eight engravings of ships. The sails remain folded in order to show-off the complexity of the rigging. One of the shields by the ship's centre mast bears the Master's housemark, a detail which, taken in the context of the other shields, provides the starting point for the theory that the engraver may be Willem vanden Cruce.

(24) *St Quirinus*
Engraving; 111:88 (borderlines), inscription cut off
Hollstein, XII, p. 215; Lehrs, VII, 20
Bequeathed by Francis Douce, 1834

St Quirinus, a Roman martyr under Hadrian, was venerated at Neuss on the Rhine after his bones were placed there by Pope Leo IX in 1050. The worshipping pilgrims have hung up votive offerings to the Saint on the left wall. During the 15th century he was one of the saints like St Sebastian and St Roch, who were invoked against the prevalent threat of plague.

From a Series of *Battles and Encampments of the Burgundian Army:*

(25) *Tent of the Horses*
At sides of tent roof: *W* and housemark; 120:190 (platemark)

(26) *Detachment of 30 Cavalrymen*
At upper centre: *W* and housemark; 130:173 (sheet)

(27) *Detachment of 28 Cavalrymen*
At upper left of centre: *W* and housemark; 135:182 (platemark)

(28) *Detachment of 10 Cavalrymen*
At upper left of centre: *W* and housemark; 130:179 (borderlines)

Engravings
Hollstein, XII, p. 218; Lehrs, VII, 26, 27, 28, 29
Bequeathed by Francis Douce, 1834

Master W with the Key creates rhythmic patterns by the ups and downs of the horses' legs and the angles of the lances. However, there is no real sense of depth since the horses appear to have no backs. The engravings are full of humorous touches such as the man waving on the back row of the *Detachment of 28 Cavalrymen*. These prints were probably made in connection with the campaigns of Charles the Bold, Duke of Burgundy (1467-1477), who pursued an aggressive foreign policy during the latter half of his reign.

Master IAM of Zwolle (*fl c.* 1470-1504)

Master IAM came from Zwolle, situated in the north of the Utrecht diocese and may be identified with the painter Jan van den Mijnnesten who was frequently recorded in Zwolle between 1462-1504[18] (no paintings have survived). Most of his prints are inscribed *Zwott* or *Zwtt* to indicate the name of the artist's town and have the intials IAM, IA or IM. On many of the prints there is also a small metalworker's drill included after the intials, which may indicate that the plates were engraved by a goldsmith after the painter's designs[19] (the initials and drill have been cut off all the Oxford prints on which they should occur). The early prints such as *The Large Calvary with the Horsemen* [cat. no. 29] were influenced by the late work of Rogier van der Weyden and Master W with the Key, while later on his style became more original and independent. The crowded compositions of *The Last Supper* and *The Arrest of Christ* [cat. nos. 31-32] show his animated approach, in which dramatic effect is heightened both by the distortion of perspective and by the rustic, crude realism of the figures (typical of the Northern Netherlands). Master IAM worked to a relatively large format, and despite the lack of stylistic unity in his oeuvre, his engraving technique remained fairly consistent throughout, using a broad and coarse manner in which certain areas are deeply gouged, tapering into small, hooked lines. His son Johan became a citizen of Zwolle in 1516 and may be the 'Master Johan the Printer', who in 1545 was paid for making impressions of prints which were probably from the copper-plates he had inherited from his father[20].

(29)★ *The Large Calvary with the Horsemen*
Engraving; 347:244 (sheet)
At upper centre, partly cut off: *Zwott*
Hollstein, XII, p. 260; Lehrs, VII, 6 (ii)
Bequeathed by Francis Douce, 1834

This engraving was probably executed during the 1480s. Master IAM gives the crowded composition a sense of depth by filling every space with a head or a limb of either a man or a horse. The number of different angles from which these are seen give the engraving vitality.

(30) *The Vision of St Bernard*
Engraving; 329:260 (borderlines)
At upper centre: *Zwtt*
Hollstein, XII, p. 270; Lehrs, VII, 15
Bequeathed by Francis Douce, 1834

The artist's interest in the rendering of architectural space is clearly evident. This is the only complete example of the engraving, although it is a late impression of the worn-out copper-plate. A study of the paper and its watermark (the print is presently stuck down) might show whether it was printed by Johan van den Mijnnesten's son in the late 1540s, or by Master IAM himself.

(31)★ *The Last Supper*
Engraving; 345:268 (borderlines), damaged at bottom
At upper centre: *Zwtt*
Hollstein, XII, p. 254; Lehrs, VII, 2
Bequeathed by Francis Douce, 1834

This engraving and the one following appear to be from an unfinished series of *The Passion*. The sculptural niche in which the scene is set suggests the designs are related to wood carvings or alabaster reliefs, which could have been used as stations of the cross around a church [compare with cat. no. 62]. The print, thought to date from *c.* 1485-90, is copied in a small silver house-altar from Salzburg of 1494, now in the Cloisters in New York[21].

(32) *The Arrest of Christ*
Engraving; 279:209 (sheet)
Hollstein, XII, p. 256; Lehrs, VII, 4
Bequeathed by Francis Douce, 1834

The sculptural effect of the engraving is accentuated by the use of dark shadows close to the picture plane which make the figures stand out in relief. Lehrs notes that this engraving was copied in 1495 by Gian Francesco da Tolmezzo in a fresco in the church of Provesano near Udine in Italy, showing how quickly and widely Netherlandish engravings were disseminated.

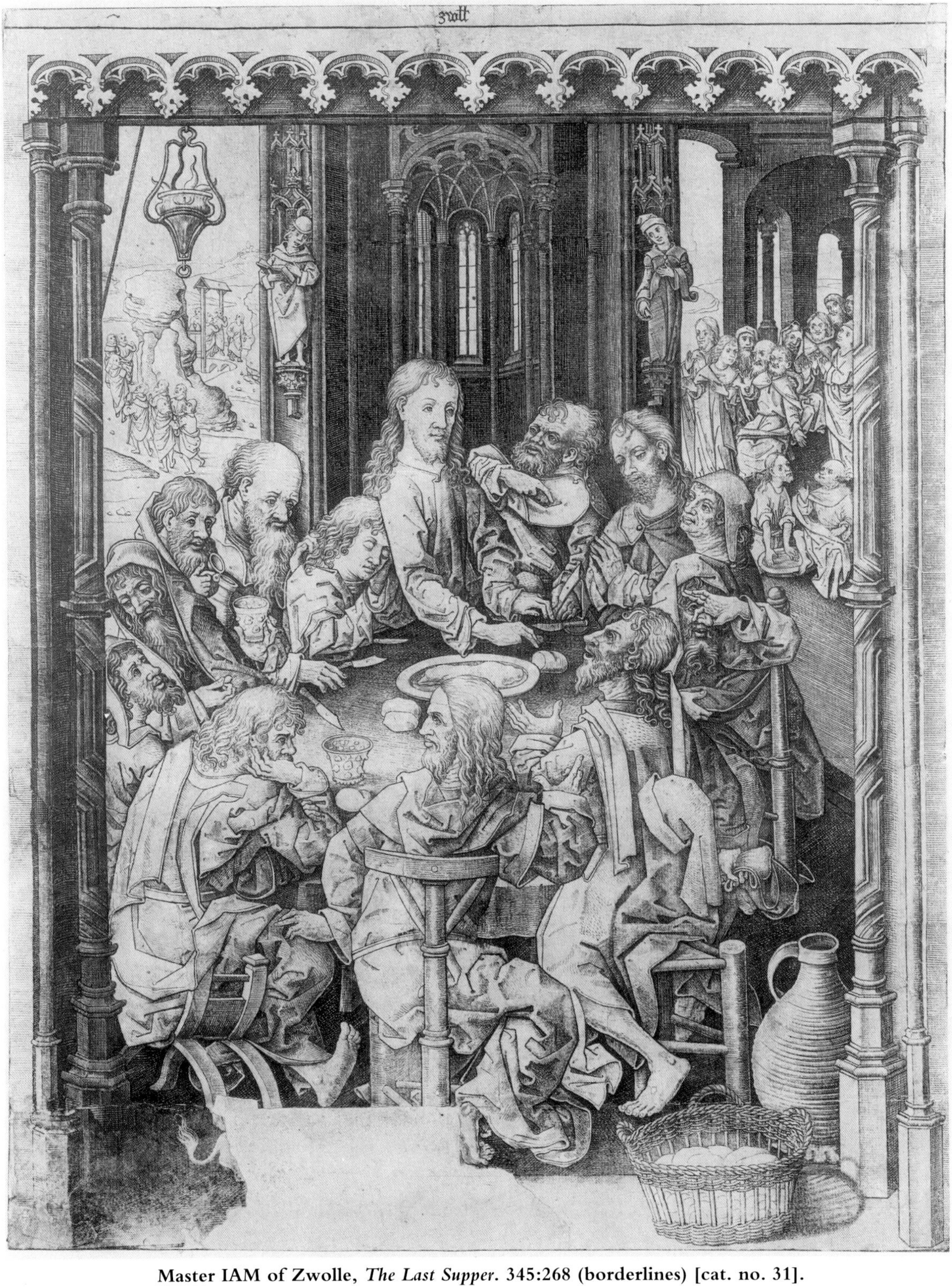

Master IAM of Zwolle, *The Last Supper*. 345:268 (borderlines) [cat. no. 31].

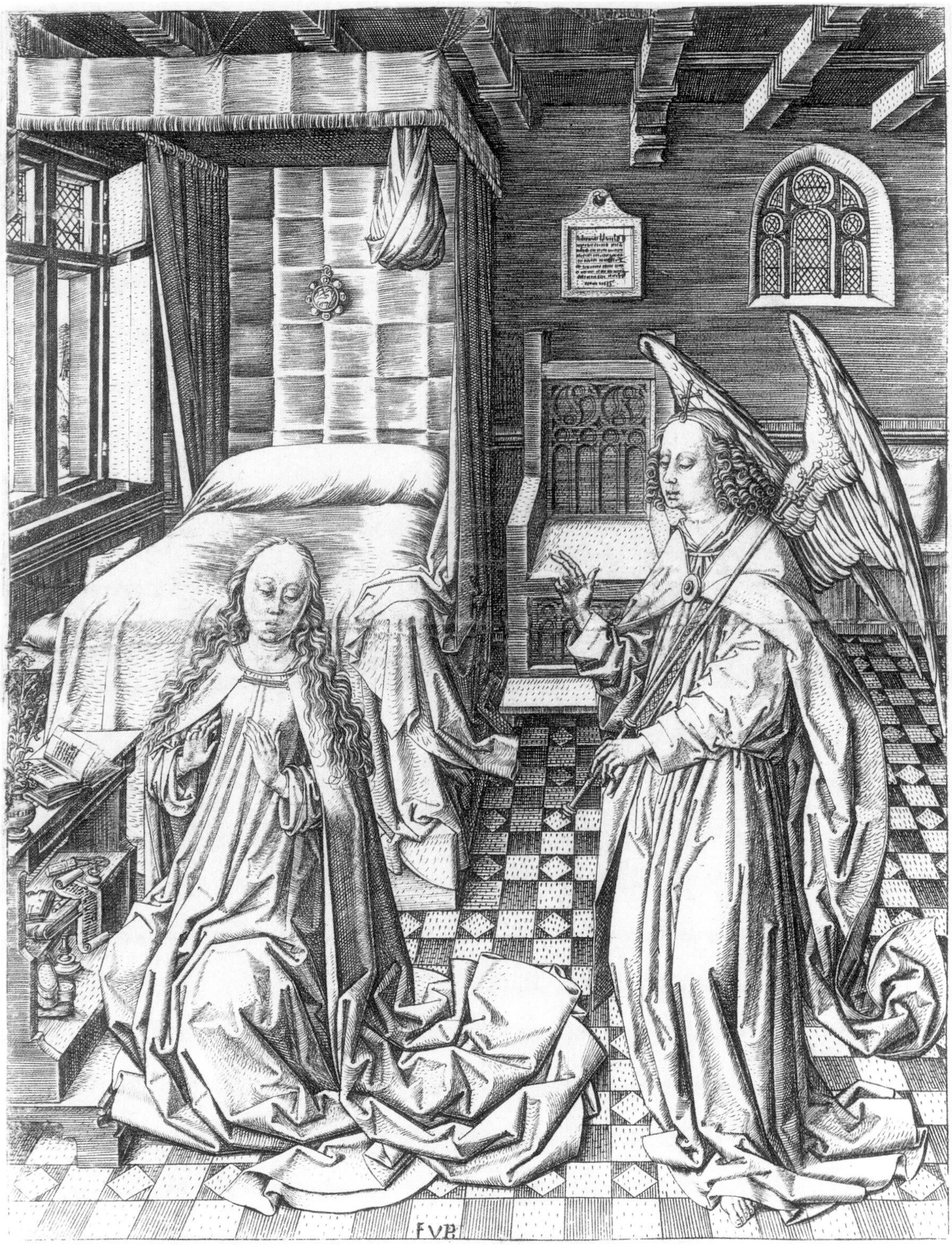

Master FVB, *The Annunciation*. 201:157 (borderlines) [cat. no. 33]. Actual size.

Master FVB (*fl c.* 1475-1500)

Master FVB was the most talented engraver working in the Netherlands in the 15th century. Primarily from his observation and copying of engravings by Martin Schongauer, he learnt how to achieve a more painterly, tonal effect than any of his Netherlandish contemporaries. His style is more angular and static than that of Schongauer, and is clearly influenced by Dieric Bouts in the use of phlegmatic, oval facial types. Stylistic connections may also be made with Rogier van der Weyden and Hans Memling. Attempts to name the artist have proved inconclusive, although it is likely that he came from Bruges.

(33)* *The Annunciation*
Engraving; 201:157 (borderlines)
At lower centre: *FVB*
Hollstein, XII, p. 144; Lehrs, VII, 4
Bequeathed by Francis Douce, 1834

This engraving is closely derived from paintings of *The Annunciation* by Rogier van der Weyden now in Paris and Munich[22]. The use of a painting as a source for the composition is further implied by the fact that the image is, as it were, in reverse: according to traditional iconography the angel should stand on the left, addressing the Virgin from her right (thought of as 'good') side. The composition may also be compared with *The Annunciation* in an early 16th-century Book of Hours by the Master of the David Scenes in the Grimani Breviary [cat. no. 60].

(34)* *The Judgement of Solomon*
Engraving; 263:217 (sheet)
At lower centre: *FVB*
Hollstein, XII, p. 141; Lehrs, VII, 2, (i)
Bequeathed by Francis Douce, 1834

This is a very fine impression of the most important engraving by Master FVB, in which even the most delicately engraved lines on the face of King Solomon are still crisp. The centre of the composition is similar to the engraving of *The Judgement of Solomon* by the Master ES [L, II, 7] and his handling of the figures is close to the style of Dieric Bouts. The Old Testament relates how Solomon adjudicated between two mothers, one whose child was dead, the other alive, but who both claimed the living child as their own. Famed for his wisdom, Solomon ordered the living child to be cut in half and divided between the two, at which point the true mother ceded her claim to the other woman, caring more for the life of her child than herself, and in so doing revealed the truth to Solomon.

(35) *Ornament with an Owl and other Birds* copy in reverse after Martin Shongauer
Engraving; 142:98 (borderlines)
At lower centre: *FVB*
Hollstein, XII, p. 167; Lehrs, VII, 59
Bequeathed by Francis Douce, 1834

Master FVB's copy is more fussy than Schongauer's original engraving [cat. no. 58] and consequently lacks clarity.

(36) *Ornament with Five Flowers*
Engraving; 95:138 (borderlines)
At lower centre: *FVB*
Hollstein, XII, p. 167; Lehrs, VII, 57
Bequeathed by Francis Douce, 1834

This ornament design is probably later than Master FVB's copy after Schongauer's *Ornament with an Owl and other Birds* [cat. no. 35] since its spacious configuration of branches, scrolling leaves and flowers suggest an awareness of the problems of printing a design which is too intricate.

(37)* *Two Peasants quarrelling over a Game of Skittles*
Engraving; 144:104 (borderlines)
At lower centre: *FVB*
Hollstein, XII, p. 164; Lehrs, VII, 51
Bequeathed by Francis Douce, 1834

This engraving is one of the earliest genre prints made in the Netherlands, forming the foundations of a tradition that culminated in the work of 17th-century artists like Adriaen van Ostade, Adriaen Brouwer, David Teniers and Rembrandt's etchings. The boorish heads and club feet of the peasants are in keeping with their loutish behaviour.

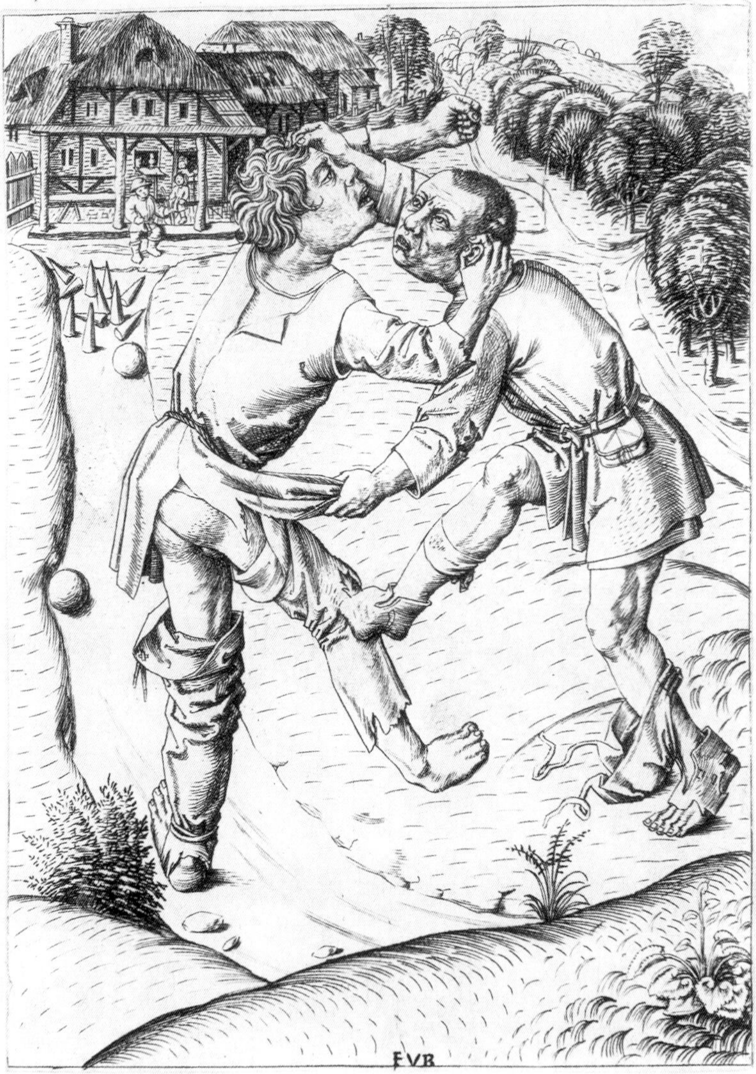

Master FVB, *Two Peasants quarrelling over a Game of Skittles*. 144:104 (borderlines)[cat. no. 37]. Actual size.

(38)* *The Monk and the Woman Spinning*
Engraving; 158:120 (borderlines)
At lower centre: *FVB*
Hollstein, XII, p. 165; Lehrs, VII, 52
Bequeathed by Francis Douce, 1834

This is probably the most unusual and violent of profane engravings to emerge from the Netherlands in the 15th century and is imbued with a strong spirit of anticlericalism against the lascivious monk. The walled yard is reminiscent of a sort of defiled *hortus conclusus* (a representation of the Virgin and Child in a walled garden, which symbolized the Virgin's chastity).

Alart Duhameel (*fl c.* 1478-1507)

Alart Duhameel is first mentioned in a contract of October 1478 as 'architect' (*Loetsmeester*), revealing that he was working on the St Janskerk in s'Hertogenbosch at the time. He was active in Leuven and Antwerp and in 1499 he was responsible for decorating the Kammerijk Hof for the reception of the Emperor Maximilian I and his son Philip, Duke of Burgundy. A year later he returned to s'Hertogenbosch for the remainder of his life. Alart Duhameel's output as an engraver was very small, eleven plates are known. It is thought the majority of these were done in the last period of his life in s'Hertogenbosch, although an engraved design for a monstrance [L, VII, 9] for the St Janskerk in s'Hertogenbosch, which was executed by the Cologne goldsmith Hendrick de Borchgrave in 1484-5, shows that Duhameel was engraving in the last quarter of the 15th century. Alart Duhameel's most popular and successful engravings were those influenced by the paintings of Hieronymus Bosch (they were both members of the Brotherhood of Our Lady in s'Hertogenbosch).

(39) *The Last Judgement*
Engraving; 241:353 (borderlines)
Hollstein, VI, p. 16; Lehrs, VII, 2 (iii)
At upper centre: *bosche* and monogram
Bequeathed by Francis Douce, 1834

Alart Duhameel inscribes the name of his town *bosche* next to his monogram at the top of the plate, in the same way as Master IAM before him inscribed *Zwott* on his plates. This appears to have been Alart's most popular print since more impressions of it survive than of any of his others (it was twice reworked). Duhameel concentrates on the hellish demons, derived from the fantastical creations of Hieronymus Bosch, rather than the trickle of Christ's faithful guided by angels up the path at the left to see Christ returning as Judge.

Perhaps by **Hieronymus Bosch (1453-1516)**

Bosch was an orthodox Roman Catholic from s'Hertogenbosch in northern Brabant, where he appears to have lived all his life. About 40 of his paintings survive revealing a strangely individual artist whose style and technique developed outside the mainstream of his contemporaries, both in terms of his surreal iconography and fluent brushwork.

(40) Double-sided Sheet of *Grotesque Studies*
Pen and bistre; 317:209
Parker, I, 23
Bequeathed by Francis Douce, 1834

Bosch's studies for his grotesque creatures are notable for their graceful lines of the quill pen, drawn swiftly and with great ease, in contrast to the closely worked silverpoint drawings which were characteristic of 15th-century draughtsmen. Alart Duhameel's engraving technique in the *Last Judgement* is reminiscent of the free lines of Bosch's drawing style, off-set by the short staccato lines in the ground which maintain the momentum of movement throughout.

Jan Gossaert, called Mabuse (*c.* 1478-1532)

Jan Gossaert was born in or near Maubeuge in the province of Hainaut (now in northern France). He was primarily a painter and was registered as a master of the Antwerp Guild of St Luke in 1503. He remained there until 1507 and in 1508 travelled to Rome with an embassy sent by Margaret of Austria, Regent of the Netherlands, to Pope Julius II. Gossaert spent almost a year in Rome, where he made pen and ink drawings of Roman antiquities and saw the work of Italian quattrocento artists and of his contemporaries, Michelangelo and Raphael. Italy had a profound effect on Gossaert, who subsequently played a central role in the Netherlandish transition from the Late Gothic style to 'Romanism', a Northern style based on antique and Italian Renaissance models. Gossaert made only three intaglio prints, all dating from the 1520s after Dürer's visit to the Netherlands.

(41)* *The Man of Sorrows*, *c.* 1525
Etching; 198:148 (borderlines)
Hollstein, VII, p. 145, 1 (i)
Bequeathed by Francis Douce, 1834

Gossaert is clearly indebted to antique models in his sculptural treatment of the figure of Christ. His departure from traditional Northern iconography and style is emphasized by the Italianate, ruined architectural setting.

Dirck Vellert (*c.* 1480-after 1547)

Dirck Vellert was chiefly a designer and painter of stained glass, his most important work being parts of the 24 stained glass windows in King's College Cambridge, commissioned by Henry VIII. Vellert was inscribed as a master of the Antwerp Guild of St Luke in 1511 and although he did paint on panel he was always referred to in the guild records as a glazier. With the exception of *The Deluge* of 1544 [cat. no. 43], all Dirck Vellert's prints were made between 1522-1526. He was one of the first Antwerp artists to make engravings and etchings following the example of Dürer and Lucas van Leyden, both of whom had experimented with etching (where the metal plate is 'bitten' in acid) as well as engraving. By combining these two methods, Vellert was able to create prints of rich texture in their hatching and stippling. Vellert was also influenced by Jan Gossaert and his prints combine both Northern and Italianate elements of style.

(42) *The Vision of St Bernard*
Engraving; 170:121 (borderlines)
At upper centre: *1524 Oct 3* (*4* in reverse)
On a slab at lower right corner: *D*V*
In cartouches on the pillars of the arched porch and on the candelabra held by putti at the top: *IHS* and *MAR*
Hollstein, XXXIII, p. 194, 8
Bequeathed by Francis Douce, 1834

St Bernard, the founder of the Cistercian Order in the 12th century, is portrayed receiving a vision of the Virgin and Child, a mystical experience which is emphasized by the chiaroscuro lighting of the figures. The Italianate architecture is set against a typically Northern, naturalistic landscape background. A stained-glass window in the church of Conches, near Evreux in France, is based on this engraving.

(43) *The Deluge*
Engraving and Etching; 268:397 (sheet)
On a slab at lower left the date: *1544* and *D*V*
Hollstein, XXXIII, p. 189, 2 (ii)
Bequeathed by Francis Douce, 1834

After an 18-year break from printmaking, Dirck Vellert returned to the medium to make his masterpiece, *The Deluge*. Almost seventy figures, many in contorted Mannerist poses, seek in vain to save themselves from the flood, through which Noah's Ark passes safely in the left background. Several of the figures appear to have been inspired by Marcantonio Raimondi's engraving *Massacre of the Innocents* [B, XIV, 19, 18]. The deep recession of the flooding landscape differs from the earlier prints and has often been compared to the mature works of the painter and tapestry-maker, Bernard van Orley.

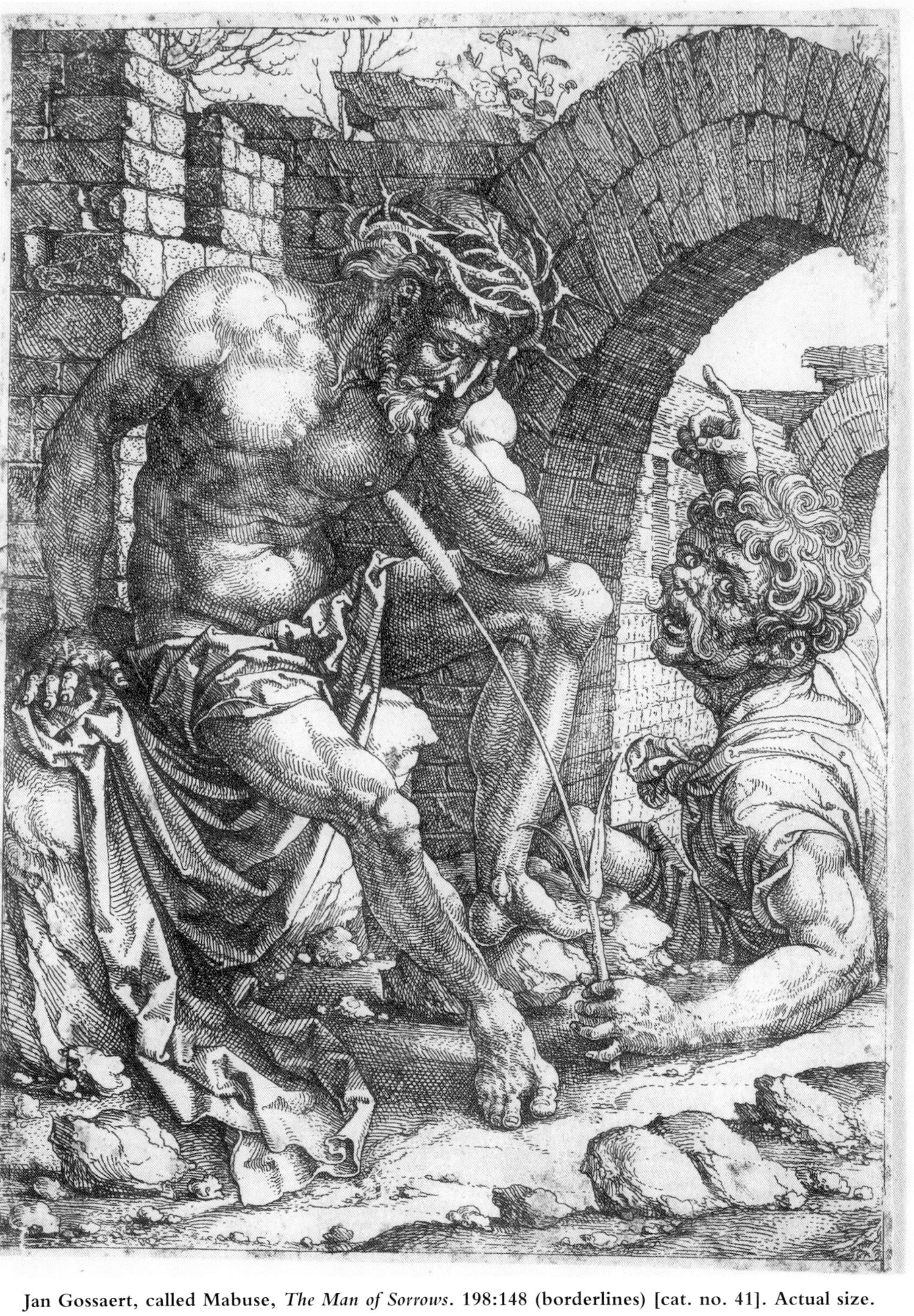

Jan Gossaert, called Mabuse, *The Man of Sorrows*. 198:148 (borderlines) [cat. no. 41]. Actual size.

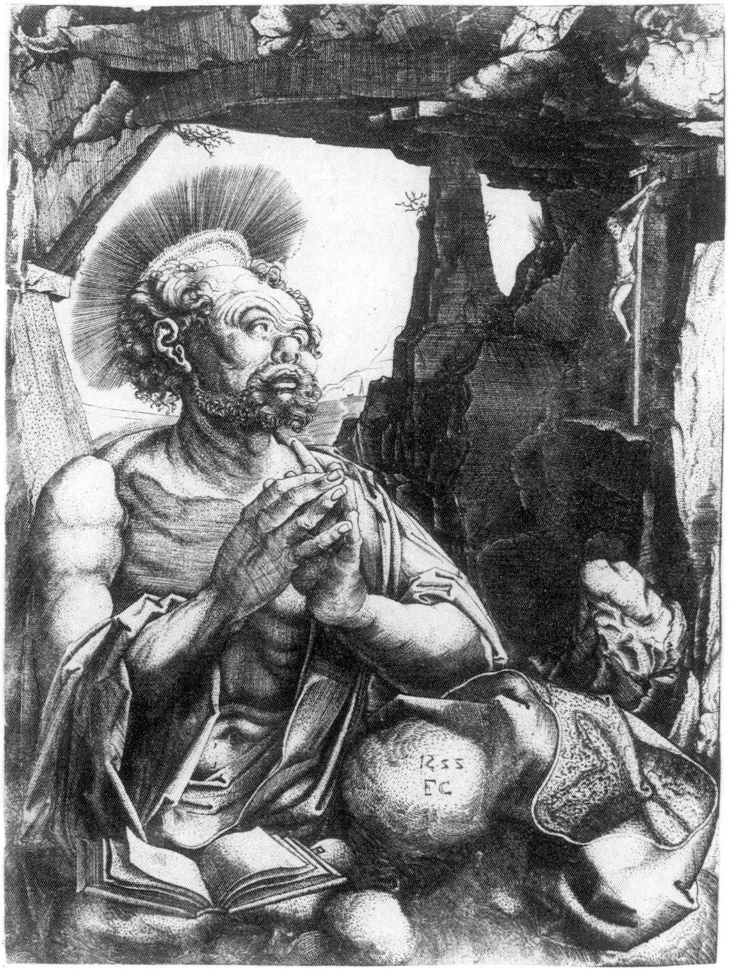

Frans Crabbe van Espleghem, *St Jerome in the Desert*. 1522. 161:122 (borderlines) [cat. no. 44].

Frans Crabbe van Espleghem (*c.* 1480–1553)

Frans Crabbe came from Mechelen, where he is recorded in the Guild of St Luke and as the head of the Brotherhood of Our Lady. He was active as an engraver, woodcutter and etcher, working in a style and technique which owed much to the Italian Renaissance, while retaining his late medieval Northern heritage in terms of subject matter. It seems likely that he would have met Dürer in June 1521, when the latter visited Mechelen. The dominant influences on his work were Lucas van Leyden, especially in his concern for atmosphere and the recession of landscape, and Jan Gossaert in his Italianate figure types.

(44)* *St Jerome in the Desert*, 1522
Engraving; 161:122 (borderlines)
In reverse at lower centre: *1522* and *FC*
H, V, p. 88, 44
Bequeathed by Francis Douce, 1834

Good surviving impressions of Frans Crabbe's prints, such as this, are very rare. The striking light, falling onto the Saint's face from behind the crucifix on which he meditates, is a characteristic feature of Crabbe's work.

Lucas van Leyden (1589(?)- 1533)

Lucas van Leyden was clearly very talented from a young age, receiving his early training from his goldsmith father, Hugo Jacobsz., and then from the Leiden painter Cornelis Engebrechtz, whose influence can first be seen in the prints dating from 1509. The work of Albrecht Dürer, almost twenty years his senior, was the most significant inspiration for Lucas van Leyden particularly in the middle years of his career. The two met in Antwerp in 1521 where they exchanged prints and Dürer made a portrait drawing of him, now in Lille. Lucas van Leyden was a prolific artist, producing at least one hundred and sixty-eight engravings in less than thirty years. This was partly due to his unusual working method: unlike Dürer who worked out a complete design before beginning to engrave, Lucas van Leyden had a free and intuitive approach, drawing lightly in drypoint straight onto the copper-plate before beginning to engrave in detail. In good early impressions one can see changes made in the creative process. During the 1510s Lucas tended to engrave his plates delicately, and to choose light-coloured, grey inks in order to achieve the tonal, atmospheric quality of Netherlandish paintings and the convincing portrayal of spatial contrasts. This technique meant that his plates wore down quickly under the pressure of the printing press with the result that first-rate impressions of his engravings are rare. During the last six years of his career Lucas van Leyden's style owed much to Jan Gossaert with whom he travelled in the Low Countries in 1527-8. Lucas's treatment of the human figure, from the elongated figures in *The Temptation of St Anthony* [cat. no. 47] to the classical nudes of *Mars, Venus and Cupid* [cat. no. 52] clearly show the change in his style and technique, becoming more graphically intense and using bold cross-hatching in the manner of Marcantonio Raimondi. Lucas van Leyden was innovative iconographically as well as technically. He preferred to depict unusual moments of well-known subjects which concentrated on debate or confusion, suspense or decision. This idiosyncratic approach was accentuated by his practice of 'inverting the narrative' as in *The Poet Virgil suspended in a Basket* [cat. no. 51]. The main events of the story are depicted in the background while the gossiping onlookers are in the foreground, as if inviting the viewer also to comment.

(45) *Mohammed and the Monk Sergius*, 1508
Engraving; 289:218 (borderlines)
On a sheet of paper at bottom left: *L*
At bottom left of centre: *1508*
The New Hollstein, p. 124, 126
Bequeathed by Francis Douce, 1834

Karel van Mander somewhat incredulously states that Lucas was only fourteen when he made this engraving. The landscape background was considered exceptionally beautiful by contemporaries and was copied by Marcantonio Raimondi[23]. The story comes from the popular anthology of tales from the East, *The Travels of Sir John Mandeville*. Mohammed's companions led him to believe that he had killed his spiritual mentor, Sergius, while he was drunk one evening. However, his drunkeness had merely sent him to sleep and so his companions had taken the opportunity of murdering the ascetic monk whom they disliked. Mohammed, conscience-struck, swore never to drink again.

(46) *Pilgrims*, *c.* 1508
Engraving; 151:120 (borderlines)
At bottom left: *L*
The New Hollstein, p. 139, 149
Bequeathed by Francis Douce, 1834

These pilgrims, resting on their journey, have devotional prints of saints heads pinned to their hats, along with the traditional symbol of pilgrims en route to Northern Spain, the shell of St James of Compostella.

(47) *The Temptation of St Anthony*, 1509
Engraving; 178:142 (sheet)
On rock at lower centre: *1509* and *L*
The New Hollstein, p. 118, 117
Bequeathed by Francis Douce, 1834

St Anthony, who renounced his rich inheritance to live as a hermit in the desert, was an example of man's power to conquer the enticements of the devil, often portrayed in the form of grotesque demons. Here,

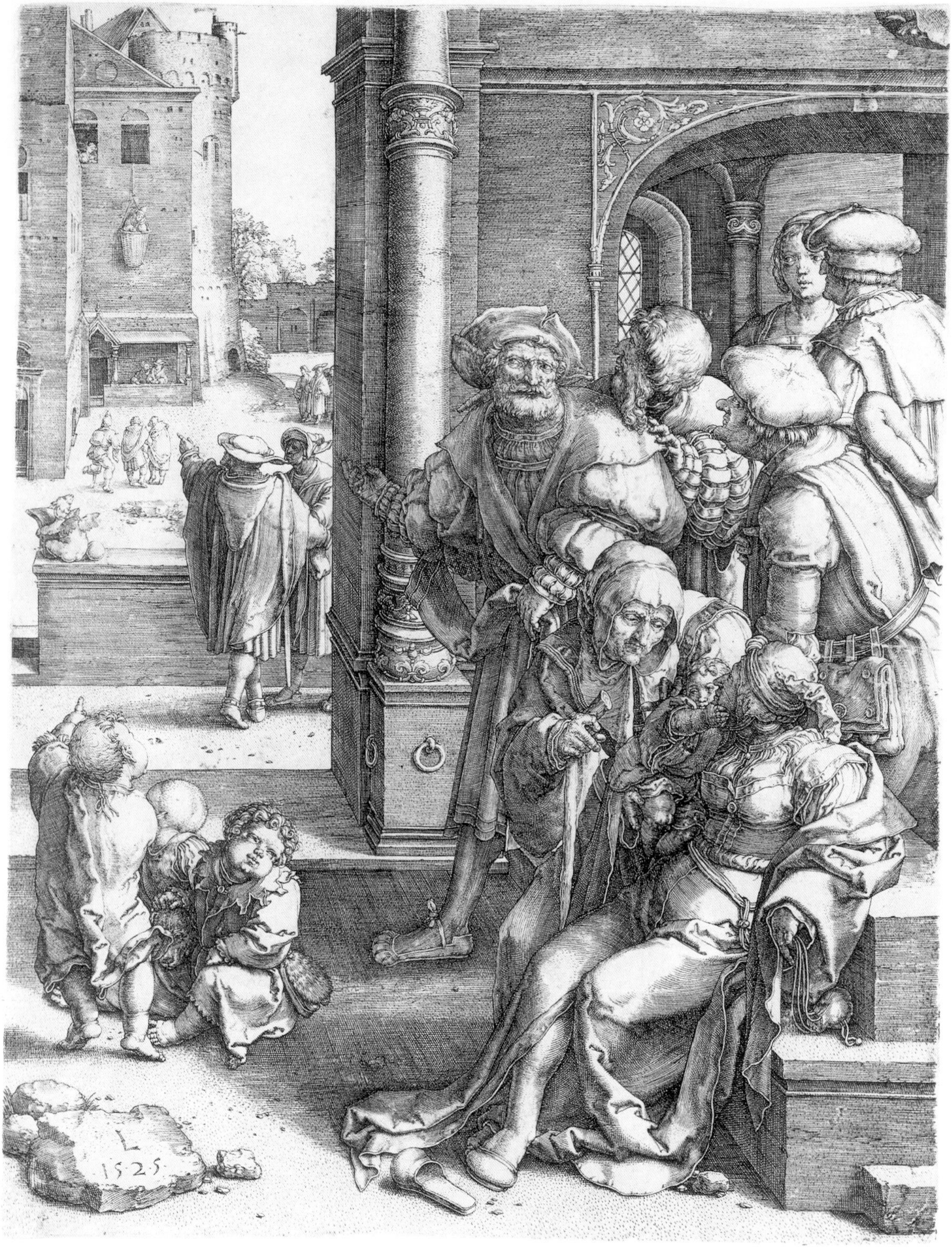

Lucas van Leyden, *The Poet Virgil suspended in a Basket*, 1525. 243:189 (borderlines) [cat. no. 51].

however, St Anthony is confronted with a single temptation more akin to daily life, a woman threatening to untie the sash around her belly, whose one devilish attribute is her horned bonnet.

(48)* *Christ appearing to Mary Magdalen as a Gardener*, 1519
Engraving; 132:167 (borderlines)
On rock at upper left: *L*;
At upper right: *1519*
The New Hollstein, p. 95, 77 (i)
Bequeathed by Francis Douce, 1834

The inspiration for this engraving came from a woodcut of the same subject by Dürer [H, VII, 156]. However, Lucas cuts off the full-length figures of Dürer's composition thus concentrating our attention on the emotional drama of Mary Magdalen recognising the risen Christ. The light diffused throughout the image gives the engraving a silvery appearance characteristic of Lucas's prints of this period.

(49) *Young Man with a Skull*, *c.* 1519
Engraving, 184:142 (borderlines)
At lower left corner: *L*
The New Hollstein, p. 157, 174
Bequeathed by Francis Douce, 1834

Tradition holds this to be a self-portrait (Karel van Mander refers to it as such), in which Lucas meditates on the pointless nature of earthly pleasures, symbolized by the juxtaposition of his extravagant plumed hat and the skull he holds, indicating the inevitable death to come.

(50)* *The Promenade*, 1520
Engraving; 113:72 (borderlines)
At upper left: *1520*
At bottom right: *L*
The New Hollstein, p. 136, 144
Bequeathed by Francis Douce, 1834

This is one of Lucas van Leyden's most charming engravings, acquiring its romantic air from the loving gaze of a wife at her husband, a unity which is accentuated by the harmonious contours of their figures as they walk. Lucas off-sets the long strokes of flowing drapery with short stippled flecks for the man's fur collar and his wife's fur-lined sleeves. The rowing boat just coming into view on the river below gives a sense of spontaneity as if the artist had captured a moment's look.

(51)* *The Poet Virgil suspended in a Basket*, 1525
Engraving; 243:189 (borderlines)
On stone at lower left corner: *L* and *1525*
The New Hollstein, p. 130, 136 (i)
Bequeathed by Francis Douce, 1834

Virgil, according to popular medieval romance, had pressed his suit on the Emperor's beautiful daughter until finally she had agreed to lift him to her chamber in a basket during the night. However, she left Virgil suspended halfway-up so that come daybreak he was the laughing-stock of Rome. The story was used as a humorous example of the folly of lustful men. This is a good impression which shows the chiaroscuro lighting of Lucas's later prints. The facial structures and finely worked raiment of the group of onlookers reveal the influence of Jan Gossaert and the artist's sense of competition with Albrecht Dürer.

(52) *Mars, Venus and Cupid*, 1530
Engraving; 189:245 (platemark)
At top right: *1530* and *L*
The New Hollstein, p. 132, 137 (i)
Bequeathed by Francis Douce, 1834

This was Lucas van Leyden's last engraving, its Mannerist style clearly paying homage to Italian Renaissance art. Mars is depicted in the moment of moral dilemma as he is confronted with the enticing availability of Venus, the Goddess of Love. The sword dividing the composition in half acts as a sort of moral boundary, which Mars's extended leg has already crossed, indicating the outcome of his desire.

(53) *St Jerome*, 1521
Black chalk with the point of the brush in dark ink, brown wash and white heightening, some lines drawn in pen and dark ink, the background in blue bodycolour; 376:281
At lower right, reinserted upside down: *L*
At lower left: *1521*
In gold lettering at centre on the left: *St Hieronemus*
Purchased, 1953.119

This finely executed drawing is signed at the lower right, although someone has cut out the *L* and reinserted it upside down. The date of 1521 is signifi-

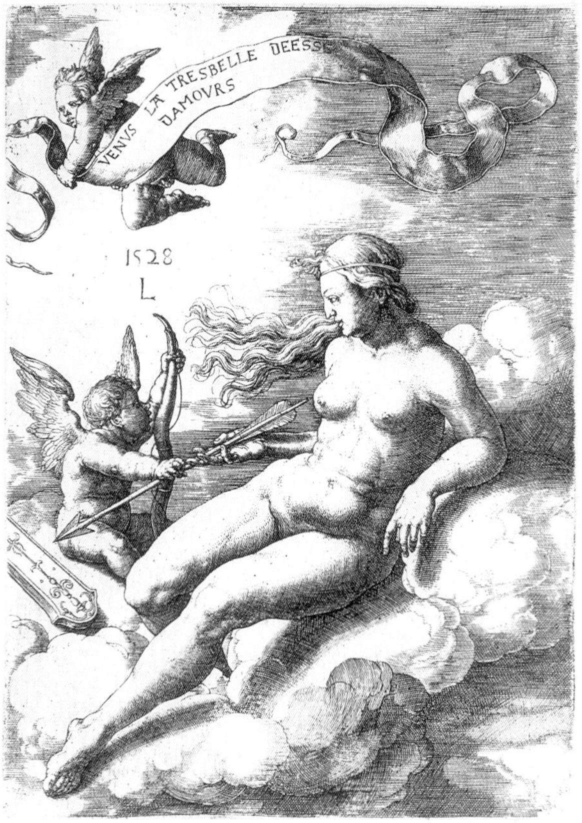

Lucas van Leyden, *Venus and Cupid*, 1528.
159:112 (borderlines) [cat no. 55].

cant since this was the year that Lucas van Leyden met Dürer in Antwerp and it was here that Dürer made his influential painting of *St Jerome*, together with preparatory drawings, to which Lucas is clearly indebted, both compositionally and stylistically. Lucas probably intended this intimate and sober drawing to be a presentation sheet. The blue background may not have been applied by the artist, but it is certainly 16th -century and is reminiscent of the backgrounds in portraits and miniatures by Hans Holbein. There are about thirty known drawings by Lucas van Leyden.

(54) *Esther before Ahasuerus*, 1518
Engraving; 277:225 (borderlines)
At lower centre: *L* and *1518*
The New Hollstein, p. 61, 31
Bequeathed by Francis Douce, 1834

This is a late impression in which the contours of the figures and the chief lines of the drapery have been reworked with the result that the outlines appear out of keeping with the rather faded descriptions of tone. Lucas enjoys teasing the viewer – surely the hand pointing the two men through the door in the top right hand corner belongs to a third person standing behind the door?

(55)* *Venus and Cupid*, 1528
Engraving; 159:112 (borderlines)
On banderole: *VENUS LA TRESBELLE DEESSE DAMOURS*
At centre on the left: *1528* and *L*
The New Hollstein, p. 133, 138
Bequeathed by Francis Douce, 1834

Lucas's interest in strong graphic contrasts towards the end of his career are manifest in this dynamic engraving. His treatment of the female form is monumental, following the classical ideals of the Renaissance. This is an early impression in which one can still see the polishing lines on the plate.

German Engravers

The most skilled masters of engraving in 15th-century Northern Europe came from Germany. Their prints travelled down the Rhine rapidly and were crucial in the technical and stylistic development of engraving in the Netherlands throughout the 15th and early 16th centuries. Master ES, Martin Schongauer and Albrecht Dürer were each the most significant of the second, third and fourth generation of engravers respectively and their achievements (especially Dürer's) have been widely celebrated over subsequent centuries.

Master ES (*fl* 1450-67)

(56) *St Michael*
Engraving; 174:130 (sheet)
Lehrs, II, 154
At upper centre: *1467*
Bequeathed by Francis Douce, 1834

The flourishing drapery of St Michael shows the innovative technique of the Master ES, who was the first master to use cross-hatching.

Martin Shongauer (*c.* 1450-1491)

(57) *The Death of the Virgin*, *c.* 1474
Engraving; 254:169 (platemark)
At lower centre: M+S
Lehrs, V, 106, 16
Bequeathed by Francis Douce, 1834

This is one of the very best impressions of this plate, in which all the finest lines, for instance on the Virgin's face, can be seen with great clarity. Schongauer perfected the technique of the Master ES by using controlled systems of hatching and cross-hatching. His aim is pictorial and tonal rather than linear.

(58) *Ornament with Owl and other Birds*, *c.* 1474
Engraving; 144:101 (borderlines)
At lower centre: M+S
Lehrs, V, 371, 115
Bequeathed by Francis Douce, 1834

This early impression appears to date from roughly the same period as *The Death of the Virgin* since the earliest impressions of both engravings may be found on paper with the same watermark[24]. The ink has pulled a little unevenly onto the paper during printing, meaning that some lines do not appear as a solid band of ink.

Albrecht Dürer (1471-1528)

(59) *Nemesis*
Engraving; 324:230 (sheet)
At lower right on a plaque: *AD*
Hollstein, VII, 66, 72; Bartsch, VII, 91, 77 (ii)
Bequeathed by Francis Douce, 1834

Few engravings illustrate so well Dürer's love of crisp linearity and grandeur in the treatment his subjects. Nemesis was credited with transferring Greek knowledge to Rome.

Manuscript

The Master of the David Scenes in the Grimani Breviary (early 16th century)

(60) *The Annunciation*
Book of Hours of the Use of Rome
Bound in worn red velvet, rebacked with two clasps (one lost)
Pächt & Alexander, vol 1, no. 397, p. 30
Oxford, Bodleian Library, MS Douce 256, fol. 48 verso

The Master of the David Scenes in the Grimani Breviary frequently used familiar compositions based on the work of earlier illuminators or painters. This miniature is derived from a painting of *The Annunciation* by Rogier van der Weyden on the left wing of the Columba Altarpiece in Munich[25] (also an important source for the engraving of *The Annunciation* by Master FVB [cat. no. 33]). The illuminator was given his long name as a result of the miniatures he painted in the Grimani Breviary, a sumptous manuscript produced in Bruges in the early 16th century, on which a number of artists worked including Jan Gossaert. It is likely that the Master was based in Bruges, where this Book of Hours was probably produced. However, it is possible that he resided in Ghent, the home of Joanna of Castile (wife of Philip the Handsome, Duke of Burgundy), whose Book of Hours he also illuminated.

Artefacts

? Flanders, *c.* 1480

(61) A Gothic Monstrance
Silver-gilt and rock-crystal; 373 mm (height)
Mark: Two indistinct gothic letter in a square punch struck on one of the reliquary terminals; French 19th-century control marks, two on foot and one on crucifixion at top.
Bequeathed by J. Francis Mallett, 1947.191.129

Monstrances were commonly kept on altars or in tabernacles in 15th-century churches. The host or relic (perhaps a bone or a piece of the saint's clothing) would have been placed inside the rock-crystal container to inspire devotion. The finial section above the display case is formed as an elaborate openwork gothic steeple, with flying butresses and pinacles. The design may be readily compared with the engraving of *A Gothic Monstrance* by Master W with the Key [cat no. 18].

? Master of Rimini (Southern Netherlandish, early 15th century)

(62) *Christ's Agony in the Garden of Gethsemane, c.* 1440
Alabaster relief; 180:210
Bequeathed by J. Francis Mallett, 1947.191.231

The carving of this relief is of high quality. It may have been made as part of a predella panel to be placed in an altar under a large Crucifixion scene[26]. Alabaster was a popular material for small-scale sculpture in Northern Europe from the late 14th century since it is a soft stone to carve. Although no engraving is known to relate to this piece it gives a good impression of how easily engraving and small-scale sculpture could relate to one another.

Coins

(63) David, Bishop of Utrecht, 1456-94
Martinsgulden
Gold, 3.00g
P. O. van der Chijs, *De munten derbisschoppen, van de heerlijkheid en de stad Utrecht*, Haarlem 1859, pl.17,10

(64) Philip the Handsome, Duke of Burgundy, 1482-1506
Florin (=goldgulden), Flanders
Gold, 3.30g
H. Enno van Gelder and M. Hoc, *Les monnaies des Pays-Bas Bourguignons et Espagnols 1434-1713*, Amsterdam, 1960, no. 115-5

(65) Philip the Good, Duke of Burgundy, 1419-1467
Double mite, Brabant
Billon, 0.84g
H. Enno van Gelder and M. Hoc, *Les monnaies des Pays-Bas Bourguignons et Espagnols 1434-1713*, Amsterdam, 1960, no. 19

(66) Philip the Good, Duke of Burgundy, 1419-1467
Mite, Brabant
Billon, 0.69g
H. Enno van Gelder and M. Hoc, *Les monnaies des Pays-Bas Bourguignons et Espagnols 1434-1713*, Amsterdam, 1960, no. 20

NOTES

1. Th. Musper, "Der Früheste Stecher – Ein Oberdeutscher", *Pantheon*, 28 (1941), pp. 203-7, argues the Master of the Death of the Virgin came from South Germany. Jan Piet Filedt Kok agrees that this is probable in his entry on the Master in the *Dictionary of Art*, (ed) Jane Turner, Macmillan, 1996.

2. see Campbell, Lorne, "The Art Market in the Southern Netherlands in the Fifteenth Century", *The Burlington Magazine*, 118 (1976), p. 196, note 112.

3. Mander, Karel van *Het Shilderboeck*, Haarlem 1604, translated and edited by Hessel Miedema, Doornspijk, 1994.

4. see Landau, David, and Peter Parshall, *The Renaissance Print 1470-1550*, New Haven and London, 1994, p. 354.

5. Boston, Museum of Fine Art, Lille, Musée des Beaux-Arts, and the collection of Mr J. P. Getty.

6. see Wim Blockmans, "The Creative Environment: Incentives to and Functions of Bruges Art Production", *Petrus Christus in Renaissance Bruges. An Interdisciplinary Approach*, (ed) Maryan W. Ainsworth, New York, Metropolitan Museum of Art, 1996, esp. pp.16-18, on the proximity of different social classes in Bruges during the period *c.* 1440-75.

7. see Landau, David, and Peter Parshall (op. cit. note 4), p. 319, on the contrast between Lucas van Leyden and Dürer in their conception of engraving.

8. British Library, Harley MS 1662, see Marrow, James "A Book of Hours from the Circle of the Master of the Berlin Passion: Notes on the Relationship between Fifteenth-Century Manuscript Illumination and Printmaking in the Rhenish Lowlands", *The Art Bulletin* (1978), pp. 591-613.

9. Rogier van der Weyden, *The Annunciation*, left wing of the Columba Altarpiece, *c.* 1450-60. Panel, 138 x 70 cm. Munich, Alte Pinakothek (inv. no. WAF 1190).

10. Matthias Quadt von Kinkelbach, *Teutscher Nation Herligkeitt: Ein außfuhrliche bechreibung des gegen wertigen/ alten/und uhralten Standts Germaniae*, Cologne: Wilhelm Lützenkirchen, 1609, pp.425-35; cited by Landau and Parshall, (op. cit. note 4), p. 354 and p. 411, note 355.

11. Bartsch, Adam, *Le Peintre-Graveur*, 21 vols, Paris, 1803-21.

12. *Douce Diary*, Bodleian Library, Oxford, MSS Douce e 66-68.

13. see note 1.

14. Geisberg, Max, *Der Meister der Berliner Passion und Israhel van Meckenem*, Strasbourg, 1903.

15. see note 8.

16. Anzelwsky, Felix, "Die drei Boccaccio-Stiche von 1476 und ihre Meister", *Festschrift Friedrich Winkler*, Berlin, 1959, esp pp. 122-125.

17. Wegener Sleeswyk, A., "De Graveur WA: Een Speurtocht", *Gens Nostra*, 49 (1994), pp. 1-13; see also Stogdon, Nicholas, "Prints from Goluchów Rediscovered", *The Print Quarterly*, 13 (1996), p.167, note 14 (I am grateful to the author for pointing this out to me).

18. Dubbe, B., "Is Johan van den Mynnesten de Meester van Zwolle'?", *Bulletin van het Rijksmuseum*, 18 (1970), pp. 55-65.

19. Filedt Kok, Jan Piet, "Master IAM of Zwoll - the personality of a designer and engraver" *Festschrift to Erik Fischer, European Drawings from six Centuries*, 1990, pp.341-56; and Stogdon, Nicholas, "Prints from Goluchów Rediscovered" *The Print Quarterly*, 13 (1996), p.168, note 18, surveys the literature.

20. Filedt Kok, Jan Piet (op. cit. note 19), p.355, note 9.

21. Filedt Kok, Jan Piet (op. cit., note 19) p. 351, fig. 10.

22. Rogier van der Weyden (or school?), *The Annunciation c.* 1435-40. Panel, 86 x 93 cm. Paris, Musée du Louvre (inv. no. 1982); see note 9 for Munich painting.

23. copied in same direction by Marcantonio Raimondi, *Bathing Soldiers*, 1510 (B. 487).

24. According to the research of Nicholas Stogdon.

25. see note 9.

26. I am grateful to Jeremy Warren for this information.

SELECT BIBLIOGRAPHY

Anzelwsky, Felix, "Die drei Boccaccio-Stiche von 1476 und ihre Meister", *Festschrift Friedrich Winkler*, Berlin, 1959.

Bartsch, Adam, *Le Peintre-Graveur*, 21 vols, Paris, 1803-21.

Blockmans, Wim "The Creative Environment: Incentives to and Functions of Bruges Art Production", *Petrus Christus in Renaissance Bruges. An Interdisciplinary Approach*, (ed.) Ainsworth, Maryan W., New York, Metropolitan Museum of Art, 1996.

Campbell, Lorne, "The Art Market in the Southern Netherlands in the Fifteenth Century", *The Burlington Magazine*, 118 (1976), pp. 188-198.

Châtelet, Albert, *Early Dutch Painting - Painting in the Northern Netherlands in the fifteenth Century*, Amsterdam, 1980.

Dubbe, B., "Is Johan van den Mynnesten de Meester van Zwolle'?", *Bulletin van het Rijksmuseum*, 18 (1970), pp. 55-65.

Filedt Kok, Jan Piet, *The New Hollstein Dutch & Flemish Etchings, Engravings and Woodcuts 1450-1700: Lucas van Leyden*, (ed.) Ger Luijten, Amsterdam, 1996.

Filedt Kok, Jan Piet, "Master IAM of Zwoll - the personality of a designer and engraver", *Festschrift to Erik Fischer, European Drawings from six Centuries*, 1990, pp.341-56.

Geisberg, Max, *Der Meister der Berliner Passion und Israhel van Meckenem*, Strasbourg, 1903.

Hollstein, F. W. H., *Dutch and Flemish Etching, Engravings and Woodcuts ca. 1450-1700*, Amsterdam, 1949–.

Jacobowitz, Ellen S., and Stephanie Loeb Stepanek, *The Prints of Lucas van Leyden and His Contemporaries,* (exh. cat.) Washington, D.C., National Gallery of Art, 1983.

Landau, David, and Peter Parshall, *The Renaissance Print 1470-1550*, New Haven and London, 1994.

Lehrs, Max, *Geschichte und kritischer Katalog des deutschen, niederländischen, und französischen Kupferstichs im XV. Jahrhundert*, 16 vols, Vienna, 1908-34.

Mander, Karel van, *Het Schilderboeck*, Haarlem 1604, translated and edited by Hessel Miedema, Doornspijk, 1994.

Marrow, James "A Book of Hours from the Circle of the Master of the Berlin Passion: Notes on the Relationship between Fifteenth-Century Manuscript Illumination and Printmaking in the Rhenish Lowlands", *The Art Bulletin* (1978), pp. 591-613.

Panofsky, Erwin, *Early Netherlandish Painting. Its origins and character*, 2 vols, Harvard University Press, 1964.

Shestack, Alan, *Fifteenth-Century Engravings of Northern Europe,* (exh. cat.) Washington D.C., National Gallery of Art, 1968.

Wegener Sleeswyk, A., "De Graveur WA: Een Speurtocht", *Gens Nostra*, 49 (1994), pp. 1-13.

Walter L Strauss, *The Illustrated Bartsch*, New York, 1978-82.

APPENDIX

Index of all the engravings and etchings (not woodcuts) by Netherlandish artists working in the period *c.* 1440-1540 in the Ashmolean Museum (not including copies)

Fifteenth Century

Master of the Death of the Virgin
H, XII, 195; L, I, 3

Master of the Berlin Passion
H, XII, 111; L, III, 115

Master of the Boccaccio Illustrations
H, XII, 119; L, IV, 4
H, XII, 120; L, IV, 5
H, XII, 121; L, IV, 7
H, XII, 121; L, IV, 8
H, XII, 122; L, IV, 10
H, XII, 116; L, IV, app 12
H, XII, 116; L, IV, app 13
H, XII, 116; L, IV, app 15
H, XII, 116; L, IV, app 16
H, XII, 116; L, IV, app 17
H, XII, 116; L, IV, app 19
H, XII, 116; L, IV, app 20
H, XII, 116; L, IV, app 21

Alart Duhameel
H, VI, 16; L, VII, 2
H, VI, 19; L, VII, 5

Master FVB
H, XII, 141; L, VII, 2i
H, XII, 144; L, VII, 4
H, XII, 156; L, VII, 40 ii
H, XII, 160; L, VII, 45
H, XII, 164; L, VII, 51
H, XII, 165; L, VII, 52
H, XII, 167; L, VII, 57

Monogrammist hos with the knife
H, XII, 183; L, VII, 1
H, XII, 183; L, VII, 4

Master IAM of Zwolle
H, XII, 254; L, VII, 2
H, XII, 257; L, VII, 4
H, XII, 260; L, VII, 6 ii
H, XII, 270; L, VII, 15

Monogrammist MG
H, XII, 189; Pass II, p.291, 1

Monogrammist P
H, XII, 190; Pass II, p.291, 1

Master W with the Key
H, XII, 205; L, VII, 3A
H, XII, 215; L, VII, 20
H, XII, 218; L, VII, 26
H, XII, 218; L, VII, 27
H, XII, 218; L, VII, 28
H, XII, 218; L, VII, 29
H, XII, 220; L, VII, 41
H, XII, 226; L, VII, 49b
H, XII, 228; L, VII, 51
H, XII, 232; L, VII, 55
H, XII, 234; L, VII, 57
H, XII, 238; L, VII, 61
H, XII, 240; L, VII, 63
H, XII, 241; L, VII, 64
H, XII, 242; L, VII, 65
H, XII, 243; L, VII, 66

Sixteenth Century

Monogrammist AT
H, XIII, 7, 8

Monogrammist AB
H, XIII, 17, 1

Monogrammist CG
H, XIII, 21, 1

Allart Claesz.
H, IV, 101, 1
H, IV, 102, 3-6
H, IV, 102, 4
H, IV, 102, 5
H, IV, 102, 6
H, IV, 103, 10
H, IV, 104, 15
H, IV, 105, 16
H, IV, 107, 24
H, IV, 115, 58
H, IV, 116, 63
H, IV, 117, 66
H, IV, 117, 67
H, IV, 117, 68
H, IV, 132, 116
H, IV, 133, 121
H, IV, 134, 123
H, IV, 136, 127
H, IV, 137, 131
H, IV, 138, 137
H, IV, 140, 143
H, IV, 140, 144
H, IV, 141, 145
H, IV, 144, 153
H, IV, 146, 159
H, IV, 146, 160
H, IV, 147, 162
H, IV, 150, 167
H, IV, 150, 168
H, IV, 150, 169
H, IV, 150, 170
H, IV, 150, 171
H, IV, 150, 172
H, IV, 150, 173
H, IV, 151, 175
H, IV, 158, 202
H, IV, 164, 226

Frans Crabbe van Espleghem
H, V, 73, 21

Jan Gossaert, called Mabuse
H, VIII, 145, 1
H, VIII, 147, 3

Monogrammist .I.S.
H, XIII, 67, 1

Nicolas Hogenberg
H, IX, 64, 73

Lucas Van Leyden
(numbers correspond with H, X, p.57 *ff.* and B, VII, but states may differ)
NH 1 i
NH 2 i
NH 3 i
NH 5 i
NH 6 i
NH 7
NH 8
NH 9
NH 13
NH 14
NH 18
NH 28
NH 29
NH 31 i
NH 32 ii
NH 33
NH 34
NH 38
NH 40 ii
NH 41 ii
NH 42
NH 46 i
NH 49 i
NH 68
NH 71 ii
NH 72
NH 73
NH 74 iii
NH 77 i
NH 79
NH 81
NH 82
NH 83
NH 84 i
NH 85
NH 101
NH 105
NH 108
NH 110
NH 113
NH 114 i
NH 117
NH 119
NH 120
NH 121
NH 122 ii
NH 123
NH 124
NH 126 i
NH 127 i
NH 135
NH 136 i
NH 137 i
NH 138 ii
NH 139 i
NH 140
NH 141
NH 142
NH 143
NH 144
NH 145
NH 147
NH 149
NH 150
NH 151
NH 153
NH 154
NH 155
NH 156
NH 157
NH 158
NH 164
NH 174 i

Monogrammist L
H, XIII, 71, 2
H, XIII, 71, 4
H, XIII, 71, 5
H, XIII, 71, 7
H, XIII, 71, 9
H, XIII, 71, 13
H, XIII, 71, 15
H, XIII, 72, 23
H, XIII, 72, 24
H, XIII, 72, 25

Master PVL
H, XIII, 117, 7

Jan van Rillaer
H, XIII, 105, 1

Master S
H, XIII, 121, 2
H, XIII, 138, 166
H, XIII, 193, 343
H, XIII, 208, 396
H, XIII, 212, 407
H, XIII, 216, 424
H, XIII, 218, 433
H, XIII, 218, 445a

Lambert Suavius
H, XXVIII, 171, 13 i
H, XXVIII, 174, 23 i
H, XXVIII, 175, 24
H, XXVIII, 180, 49 i

Dirck Vellert
H, XXXIII, 189, 2 ii
H, XXXIII, 190, 3 ii
H, XXXIII, 191, 4 ii
H, XXXIII, 192, 5 ii
H, XXXIII, 193, 6 i
H, XXXIII, 194, 7
H, XXXIII, 194, 8
H, XXXIII, 197, 9
H, XXXIII, 197, 10
H, XXXIII, 198, 11
H, XXXIII, 198, 12
H, XXXIII, 200, 16
H, XXXIII, 201, 17

Jan Cornelisz.Vermeyen
H, XXXVI, 117, 4
H, XXXVI, 120, 7